"In 1952 Lewis disclosed that writing his *magnum opus* on the literature of the sixteenth century had been his 'top tune' for fifteen years and all the other books he wrote during that period were 'only its little twiddly bits.' It may surprise some readers to hear Lewis describe *The Lion, the Witch and the Wardrobe, The Screwtape Letters* and *The Abolition of Man*—to mention just three—as mere twiddly bits in comparison with the main melody of his output. But that was how he saw it. Neal and Root are to be commended for rehabilitating that 'top tune' and other similarly neglected works in this clear, useful, and informative survey."

—**Michael Ward,** University of Oxford, co-editor of *The Cambridge Companion to C. S. Lewis*

"Neal and Root have done us a great service. At a time when we are in danger of being surfeited by the endless rehashing of the well-known C. S. Lewis, they have opened up the treasures of the less known but invaluable Lewis. I found this book delightful and stimulating."

—**Os Guinness,** author of *Carpe Diem Redeemed*

"Reading *The Neglected C. S. Lewis* reminded me, a professor at a very secular Russian university, of what Lewis said about Charles Williams' lecture on Milton's *Comus*: 'I have at last, if only for once, seen a university doing what it was founded to do: teaching wisdom.'"

—**Olga B. Lukmanova,** Nizhny Novgorod State Linguistics University, Russia

"I remember my surprise and delight when I discovered, as a literature student, that the author whose Narnia stories I had enjoyed as a child was also a brilliant literary critic, in fact the most lucid and helpful of all the scholars whose works I read at Cambridge. I am delighted, therefore, to see that Neal and Root are sharing so much of this treasure in this new volume. They are ideal guides. I heartily recommend this volume."

—**Malcolm Guite,** author, poet, and Chaplain at Girton College, Cambridge

"Neal and Root do not want C. S. Lewis' neglected works to remain neglected. The reasons they spell out in this book are compelling, as is the authoritative guidance they provide for those works. Beyond *Screwtape*, *Narnia*, *Mere Christianity*, and the space trilogy, there turns out to be a vast terrain of underappreciated insight (from Lewis and these authors both)."

—Mark Noll, author of *Turning Points: Decisive Moments in the History of Christianity*

"Lewis's most popular books are rich in wisdom and wonder, but many of his most important insights are buried in the pages of his lesser-known works. Now, at last, Mark Neal and Jerry Root have provided us with a map that leads us straight to the heart of these treasures."

—Diana Pavlac Glyer, Professor in The Honors College at Azusa Pacific University and author of *The Company They Keep: C. S. Lewis and J. R. R. Tolkien as Writers in Community*

"Neal and Root are reliable guides to the professional writings of C. S. Lewis, demonstrating how his insights on past literature help us navigate the turbulent waters of today's words and rhetoric."

—Bruce R. Johnson, General Editor, *Sehnsucht: The C. S. Lewis Journal*

"C. S. Lewis has two sets of readers who almost never talk to each other. Finally, Neal and Root have arisen to help introduce them to each other. It's about time!"

—Donald T. Williams, R. A. Forrest Scholar & Professor of English, Toccoa Falls College

"Even though the subject matter may seem obscure and academic, I believe that you will find your horizons broadened. The best outcome for this book will be an impetus to go back and read Lewis's 'neglected' books and the works that inspired them."

—Art Lindsley, Vice-President of Theological Initiatives at The Institute for Faith Work and Economics

The Neglected

C.S. Lewis

Exploring the Riches of His Most Overlooked Books

Mark Neal and Jerry Root

Foreword by Dr. David C. Downing
Co-Director, Marion E. Wade Center

mount
tabor
BOOKS

PARACLETE PRESS
BREWSTER, MASSACHUSETTS
BARGA, ITALY

To Reba and Isla
with all my love.
—Mark

To Tim and Marcia Tremblay,
cherished friends.
—Jerry

2020 First Printing

The Neglected C. S. Lewis: *Exploring the Riches of His Most Overlooked Books*

Copyright © 2020 by Mark Edward Neal and Gerald Richard Root

ISBN 978-1-64060-294-6

The Mount Tabor Books name and logo (mountain with rays of light) are trademarks of Paraclete Press, Inc.

Library of Congress Cataloging-in-Publication Data

Names: Neal, Mark, 1973- author. | Root, Jerry, author. | Downing, David C., writer of foreword.
Title: The neglected C.S. Lewis : exploring the riches of his most overlooked books / Mark Neal and Jerry Root ; foreword by Dr. David C. Downing, co-director, Marion E. Wade Center.
Description: Brewster, Massachusetts : Paraclete Press, [2020] | Includes bibliographical references. | Summary: "The authors trace the signature ideas in Lewis's works of literary criticism and show their relevance to Lewis's more familiar books"-- Provided by publisher.
Identifiers: LCCN 2019057349 (print) | LCCN 2019057350 (ebook) | ISBN 9781640602946 (trade paperback) | ISBN 9781640602953 (mobi) | ISBN 9781640602960 (epub) | ISBN 9781640602977 (pdf)
Subjects: LCSH: Lewis, C. S. (Clive Staples), 1898-1963--Criticism and interpretation. | Lewis, C. S. (Clive Staples), 1898-1963--Knowledge--Literature.
Classification: LCC PR6023.E926 Z7987 2020 (print) | LCC PR6023.E926 (ebook) | DDC 828/.91209--dc23
LC record available at https://lccn.loc.gov/2019057349
LC ebook record available at https://lccn.loc.gov/2019057350

10 9 8 7 6 5 4 3 2 1

Published by Paraclete Press
Brewster, Massachusetts
www.paracletepress.com

Printed in the United States of America

Contents

Foreword

When I was pursuing my doctorate in English at UCLA, various professors of mine required me to read C. S. Lewis's *The Allegory of Love*, *The Discarded Image*, *A Preface to Paradise Lost*, and *An Experiment in Criticism*. None of these professors were Christians, as far as I know, and none had any interest in Lewis the lay theologian or Lewis the fiction writer. They simply wanted me to be familiar with these classic works of literary history and criticism.

Outside of academia, though, the situation seems to be reversed. Readers who can quote word for word from *Mere Christianity* or *Perelandra* have often never read Lewis's work as a professional literary historian; they may not even recognize the titles listed above. Mark Neal and Dr. Jerry Root have done students of Lewis a great service in the pages that follow, tracing the signature ideas in Lewis's works of literary criticism and showing their relevance to Lewis's more familiar books. Their thorough research and lucid prose will be welcome to readers who would like to understand Lewis more fully, but who feel daunted by books of such evident scholarly erudition.

Lewis was a man of many parts: a medieval and Renaissance historian who wrote humorous light verse; an influential critic who wrote letters to children; a compelling Christian apologist who wrote science fiction and fantasy. Yet one always senses in Lewis's books "the one in the many." His unique sensibility, his characteristic habits of thought and mind, developed early in life and remained remarkably consistent. So there is an intriguing interconnectedness in all his books, including his scholarship. As his lifelong friend Owen Barfield once observed, reading anything by Lewis reminds you of everything else he wrote.

Lewis's mind was capacious, but it was not compartmentalized. When he produced literary scholarship, he did not cease to be a Christian. When he wrote science fiction or fantasy, he did not cease to be a medievalist. So reading any book by Lewis illuminates his other books. When you read *The Discarded Image* on the ancients' view of the heavens, you understand better why Ransom has such unpleasant sensations when first descending toward Malacandra in *Out of the Silent Planet*. And when you come across Lewis's discussion in *OHEL* of a minor sixteenth-century poet who described the hellish River Styx as a "puddle glum," you can't help but chuckle at the name when you meet the famous Marshwiggle in *The Silver Chair*.

Lewis's literary criticism illuminates a great deal more than literature. In guiding readers through so many great books, Lewis ranges into cultural history, philosophy, theology, linguistics, and even sociology and psychology. He uses Mr. Badger in *The Wind in the Willows* to explain English social history, and he refers to the historical Puritans to illustrate what is wrong with so much contemporary criticism: "The Puritan conscience works on without the Puritan theology—like millstones grinding nothing; like digestive juices working on an empty stomach and producing ulcers."

Lewis simply could not produce dull writing, even in his most scholarly tomes. His perceptivity, wit, and memorable turns of phrase appear as much in his academic writing as in his most popular works. This is not to say, of course, that Lewis's professional works are just as accessible to lay readers as his more widely read books. Readers do indeed owe a debt of gratitude to Mark Neal and Dr. Jerry Root for elucidating these classic works by Lewis and for inviting readers not to neglect these books any longer.

—Dr. David C. Downing
Co-Director, Marion E. Wade Center
Wheaton, Illinois

Introduction
Why Neglected?

Calling C. S. Lewis a neglected author would appear to be a contradiction, given the popularity of his works and their high level of awareness among Christians and non-Christians alike. One could argue that he is, in fact, more popular now than he was during his lifetime. His mainstream theological and apologetic works continue to be in high demand and *The Chronicles of Narnia* have joined the canon of classic children's literature, not to mention the feature films of recent years that have made these works and Lewis a household name. There are more scholars writing about Lewis, more societies and groups springing up around Lewis's ideas, and more books being published about him and his work, than ever before. So how do we justify this seemingly incongruous designation of "neglected"?

Within Lewis's corpus of published work are fifteen books of literary criticism (depending on how you count them) that most people don't know about or haven't read. Even people who claim to know Lewis well are often not acquainted with them. This book examines eight of Lewis's works of literary criticism. They deal with authors and literary periods that most people don't read anymore, and they are drawn primarily from Lewis's works in literary criticism, the area of his focused academic and professional work. Lewis was a fellow at Oxford University and later the Professor of Medieval and Renaissance English Literature at Cambridge University, and many of his literary loves and preoccupations are detailed in the pages of these books. So it is to these works that we apply the appellation of "neglected."

One reason for their neglect, then, is that readers of Lewis simply don't know they exist. Most mainstream attention focuses on the highly recognizable Lewis works such as his fiction and apologetics. While some of these more obscure works continue to be printed and available, others have slipped out of print and are only obtainable in rare editions or on superannuated library shelves where they sit and gather dust. They have suffered from a lack of promotion; that is, they have not been placed prominently before the reader of Lewis. Online searches of popular Lewis topics don't often yield mentions of these works, and scholars, writers, and lecturers often don't refer to them.

Another reason for this neglect is the difficulty of these works for mainstream audiences who don't possess the specialized knowledge that Lewis presupposes in his writing. Many of these books began as lectures to students or groups who already understood the context of the literature. This made such lectures intelligible. It was entirely feasible for Lewis to assume that his auditors had read the works and authors on which he was discoursing or at least had a familiarity with them or the literary periods to which they belonged. For most of us now, this familiarity is entirely lacking, and this makes the reading of these books arduous and confusing. But if we are willing to learn and read slowly and do some research along the way, they will open their secrets to us.

Fascinatingly, Lewis himself wrote about neglected authors and literary periods. He engaged in what he termed rehabilitation, defending and/or reconceptualizing a period, genre, or author for which appreciation or critical understanding had been lacking. Thus, it is our goal to do for Lewis what he did for many authors and genres: dusting off his neglected books to bring them back into the arena of attention they deserve.

A lack of interest in the content of these works might be another reason why they are neglected. Because they primarily describe specific literary historical periods and their associated works of literature, it's less an issue of them not being comprehensible as it is of them not being valued as worthy of study. In an age where the liberal arts are dwindling across college campuses in favor of more technical majors that presuppose to equip people better for the modern workplace, the kind of historical study Lewis advocates is not as appreciated as it once was. Our culture esteems actionable information over the kind of knowledge to be gained from reading the literature of another age. It's a challenge, in an age where everything changes constantly and the pace of life seems ever-increasing, to think that old works of literature can matter in any substantial way. We tend to overvalue whatever is new and conflate this with progress. These are more difficult obstacles to overcome for the would-be reader of Lewis's neglected works.

Benefits of Reading the Neglected Works

There are a number of benefits to the reader for undergoing the rigor these works demand. First of all, you'll gain a greater understanding of C. S. Lewis as a person. We believe that you can't claim to know him if you don't know these neglected works. Part of understanding any author is to understand his body of work, his preoccupations, the books he read, and so forth. Many of the works Lewis writes about were vitally important not only to his profession, but to his spiritual growth. Reading literature was a way of life.

A second benefit is that these books will lead you to other authors of which you were perhaps unaware. Lewis opens doors for us and bids us enter. If we let them, these works and the books and authors to which they lead will constitute an education in itself. For example, when one first picks up *A Preface to Paradise Lost*, one realizes that the book won't make sense unless Milton's poem is read in conjunction with it. Lewis opens this door for readers to become acquainted with Milton and one of the greatest epic poems in the English language. Similarly, his essays on Sir Walter Scott or Jane Austen can help illuminate something of Scott's or Austen's preoccupations and inform the reading of those authors' novels.

A third benefit is that these neglected works contain the development of many of Lewis's most important ideas. These ideas can frequently be found in his mainstream books, including his fiction. But they were often first formulated in his literary criticism. For example, we believe that you can't really know *The Chronicles of Narnia* or the Ransom trilogy if you haven't read *The Discarded Image*, Lewis's opus on the medieval cosmology and worldview. Doing so will enrich and deepen your understanding of those books. Similarly, reading *Studies in Words* prepares you for better understanding portions of *That Hideous Strength*. And Lewis is good at this. He creates imaginative maps of the past that enable us to imaginatively inhabit other times. He calls this inhabiting the historical imagination. He writes that we must become, for example, an eighteenth-century Londoner while reading Samuel Johnson, or an Achaean chief while reading Homer.[1] Only then will we be able to judge historical works as they were written. This

---

1 Lewis, *A Preface to Paradise Lost* (New York: Oxford University Press, 1954), 63.

keeps us from misreading, from projecting our own worldview onto a work, and not reading it the way the author intended.

Thus, another reason we should not neglect these works is that they help us avoid what Lewis termed "chronological snobbery" or the valuing of one age over another. Each age tends to devalue previous ages as shortsighted, or perhaps, as backward. But valuing all ages enables us to see our own age more clearly and to better interpret it. No conception of the future will be feasible without an understanding of the past, and a proper use of the historical imagination allows just that.

It strikes us that our current age views itself in many ways as the apotheosis of the historical continuum. The past is devalued as a means to informing the future. But it was Isaac Newton who said, "If I have seen further it is by standing on the shoulders of giants." Lewis writes to encourage this same sort of respect for, and accurate judgment of, the past. He writes that these things keep the palliative "clean sea breeze of the centuries" blowing through our minds against the characteristic blindness of the twenty-first century.[2]

Yet another benefit of reading Lewis's neglected works is that they widen our vision. Lewis writes that we read old literature because it can "re-admit us to bygone modes of thought and enable us to imagine what they felt like, to see the world through our ancestors' eyes."[3] Why is this important? Lewis writes in *An Experiment in Criticism* that we live in a narrow prison of self. We need others' eyes in order to apprehend reality and expand our understanding—this means not only the voices of the present, but those of the past as well. In opening doors to other historical times and works, Lewis is giving us these eyes. This kind of vision allows us to engage our current cultural situations more effectively and enriches our own understanding and perception of the world.

---

2 Lewis, Introduction to *St. Athanasius on the Incarnation* (London: A. R. Mowbray & Co., 1963), 5.
3 Lewis, *Studies in Medieval and Renaissance Literature*, "Edmund Spenser" (New York: Cambridge University Press, 2007), 138.

We need to be awake to our current situation so we can best be prepared as Christians to confront culture ethically rather than retreat from it, and so we don't get lulled back to sleep by the siren song of culture. In speaking of our ability to be perceptive, Lewis notes,

> [Y]ou and I have need of the strongest spell that can be found to wake us from the evil enchantment of worldliness which has been laid upon us for nearly a hundred years. Almost our whole education has been directed to silencing this shy, persistent, inner voice; almost all our modern philosophies have been devised to convince us that the good of man is to be found on this earth.[4]

Waking up is crucial to our spiritual and moral education. The study of the literature of the past keeps us sharp, develops virtue, and keeps our faith from suffering from the same soporific, lulling effect. The open doors Lewis invites us to go through can help keep us sharp and awake and imaginatively engaged.

These neglected works open onto new vistas, new modes of thought and understanding that enable us to see the world, as poet Gerard Manley Hopkins writes, that is "charged with the grandeur of God." Lewis writes that "We may ignore, but we can nowhere evade, the presence of God. The world is crowded with Him. He walks everywhere incognito."[5] Lewis sensed this richness and this deep delight in God's revelation of beauty in every sphere of life. For him, this delight was most often found in literature. Thus, as he throws wide the doors of his own pleasure in words, language, and the imaginative creation of past centuries, we can better see the world that is crowded with God. As Eric Liddell of the popular film *Chariots of Fire* said, "God made me fast. And when I run, I

---

4 Lewis, *The Weight of Glory and Other Addresses* (New York: Simon & Schuster, 1996), 29.
5 Lewis, *Letters to Malcolm: Chiefly on Prayer* (New York: Harcourt, Brace & World, 1964), 75.

feel his pleasure." We might similarly say of Lewis that God made him an astute critic of literature, and in that exercise he reveled in God's pleasure. It is clear from many of Lewis's writings that he keenly felt this unique pleasure given to him by great literature. These works are a passing on of that pleasure that we might likewise partake in it.

Finally, Lewis writes that most of his books are evangelistic: "What we want is not more little books about Christianity," he writes, "but more little books by Christians on other subjects—with their Christianity *latent*."[6] Similarly, G. K. Chesterton wrote that he didn't become a Christian because one or two things proved it to be true; he became a Christian because everything seemed to point to its truth. Lewis is often quoted along these lines when he wrote, "I believe in Christianity as I believe that the Sun has risen, not only because I see it, but because by it I see everything else."[7] He saw, and the readers of this book should see, that faith can be strengthened by a widening of the Christian worldview.

Thus, Lewis provides a model of faith integration. In a secular age we tend to compartmentalize our lives, including our faith. We don't understand how to integrate faith with the rest of what we do. Lewis serves as a model of how to integrate faith into all facets of life. He also challenges secularists to attempt a similar integration by means of whatever worldview they happen to be endorsing at any given time. In books like *The Discarded Image* he shows that ideologies and worldviews come and go, but the Christian worldview has withstood 2,000 years of distractions and opponents and continues to flourish. It was Lewis's contention that throughout the ages, the truth of Christianity was able to make sense of the greatest amount of material.

6 Lewis, *God in the Dock*, "Christian Apologetics" (Grand Rapids, MI: Eerdmans, 1970), 93.
7 Lewis, *The Weight of Glory*, "Is Theology Poetry?" 106.

Overview of the Neglected Works

This book examines eight works by Lewis that we have termed "neglected." Each chapter focuses on one work, and the book is organized chronologically according to their original publication dates. For the student of Lewis who would like to take these studies even further, in an appendix we have also included additional works that we were not able to include here.

The Allegory of Love traces the development of the medieval love allegory as Lewis follows it through the seminal works of an age. He follows the code of chivalry with its emphasis on courage, humility, the religion of love, and adultery. This was the book that established Lewis's academic reputation.

The Personal Heresy is a debate between Lewis and Elizabethan literary scholar E. M. W. Tillyard over whether or not the personality of the author needs to be known in order to interpret his or her work.

Arthurian Torso examines a cycle of poems telling the story of Camelot from the perspective of the Court Poet, Taliessin, written by Lewis's friend and fellow Inkling, Charles Williams. The poems are not easily accessible, but the theology and literary point of view is scintillating. As Dante needed a Virgil to guide him through the inferno, so the average reader needs a guide through the thought of Charles Williams.

English Literature in the Sixteenth Century excluding Drama was Lewis's magnum opus. It is the ripe fruit of an eighteen-year project that occupied much of his mind and thought. To produce this book, Lewis read every book written in English in the sixteenth century, as well as every book translated into English at that time. It not only reveals the depth of Lewis's thought, and his brilliant and winsome literary style, but the breadth of his grasp and understanding. Furthermore, this book reveals the background of the full and fertile mind that Lewis brought to all of his other work. It is an important book in the Lewis corpus and one that serious Lewis readers ought to know about.

Studies in Words examines word histories and how their meanings develop over time. Understanding their development is a source of rich treasure. The finding of treasure often requires a map, so Lewis provides that map for all who want to understand the literature beyond their own age. This guidebook helps us better understand old books through knowing the original meanings of words as well as the elements that contribute to change in meaning in language. It also details Lewis's approach to responsibility with regard to language.

Written toward the end of Lewis's life, *An Experiment in Criticism* represents his mature literary critical thought. He analyzes a book based on how it is read rather than simply judging it to be good or bad. He divides readers into two categories: receivers and users. The work examines the difference between books that produce receivers whose lives are enriched forever because of their encounter with these texts and those who remain merely users of literature and miss out on its riches. This book shows how literary experience can widen our views and enrich our understanding of the world.

The Discarded Image is the final edition of a series of lectures Lewis gave at Oxford University titled *The Prolegomena to Medieval and Renaissance Literature.* One of the last things he wrote before he died, it was published in the year following his death. This work is indispensable to knowing the background of medieval literature and to understanding Lewis's fascination with that period. Lewis shows that the medieval worldview could not be a last word about reality, and we see in this book a warning that the worldview of any age must equally give way to the demands of new discoveries. All ages will produce what will necessarily become discarded images, interesting in their own right, but insufficient to describe the full complexity of the world in which we find ourselves. This work also provides an essential key to understanding and appreciating Lewis's fiction.

This brings us to *Selected Literary Essays*. Throughout the essays in this book that is little read today, we see how, for Lewis, questions lead to answers which lead to discoveries. This promotes awe and wonder and sometimes, in Lewis's case, worship. The book shows the width of his tastes, and anybody who wants to break out of narrow self-referential approaches to life would benefit from these essays.

It is our hope that *The Neglected C. S. Lewis* will serve as a starting point to whet the interest of those who love C. S. Lewis but are not familiar with these works. Our goal is to give you some of the tools for thinking about his diverse writings in new ways. We hope that it will begin to fill the vacancy that a lack of promotion and awareness has created and will revitalize interest in the ideas contained within the books. We urge you to be open to the difficulty of the content, to be patient with the slow process of reading, re-reading, making notes, and doing additional research. We can attest that these works are worth it not only because of the value in better understanding Lewis, but to open up new worlds and ideas to be explored that can deepen our faith and give us, as Lewis writes, the ability to see with others' eyes so that our own worlds may be widened.

Lewis's renown was a consequence of his capacity to sequester himself
in focused study and academic work.

Magdalen College, Oxford, from Addison's Walk, where Lewis was a Fellow and Tutor in English Literature from 1925 to 1954.
Photo courtesy of Mark Neal.

Chapter 1

The Glory of the Ideal

The Allegory of Love

Norman Cantor, former Rhodes Scholar, Fulbright Professor and medievalist at New York University, wrote *Inventing the Middle Ages* in which he considers the influence of twenty twentieth-century medieval scholars. By his standards of assessment, he places C. S. Lewis and J. R. R. Tolkien at the top of the list. He observes, "Of all medievalists of the twentieth century, Lewis and Tolkien have gained incomparably the greatest audience, although 99.9 percent of their readers have never looked at their scholarly work."[8] And, of Lewis, he notes that "He had

8 Norman F. Cantor, *Inventing the Middle Ages: The Lives, Works, and Ideas of the Great Medievalists of the Twentieth Century* (Cambridge, UK: Lutterworth, 1991), 207.

established his reputation as a leading medieval literary historian with *The Allegory of Love* (1936)."[9] Before the publication of this book, Cantor says:

> No one in the English-speaking world had up to then the learning, insight, and courage to attempt such a sophisticated definition of high medieval culture. There had been valuable discussions of particular poets and treatises on philosophy and theology. But Lewis tried to define the essence of twentieth-century literary imagination and did so in a formula that has withstood the challenge of a half century of research and reflection.[10]

In fact, Cantor observes that "Lewis saw more deeply into medieval culture than the neo-Thomists did." Here it is worthy to note that while many of the interpreters of the development of intellectual history tend to follow the philosophers and theologians, Lewis propounds the merit of following the ideas that develop along literary lines. Furthermore, the medieval imagination—as Lewis summed it up near the end of his life—"is not a transforming imagination like Wordsworth's or a penetrating imagination like Shakespeare's. It is a realizing imagination." Cantor adds that while "Lewis left a great many questions unanswered or even unasked about the nature of the Middle Ages . . . what he had to say was persuasive and largely incontestable."[11]

The Allegory of Love is Lewis's monumental work about the medieval love allegory, and he traces developments in the literature of that age, moving from the celebration of adultery to literature that elevates the Christian ideal of marriage and holds it in high regard. He looks at some of the most significant medieval texts in order to mark this development. There is much of ancillary value

9   Cantor, 206.
10   Cantor, 214.
11   Cantor, 216.

in Lewis's exploration, but this development toward a Christian view of marriage was Lewis's main point in *The Allegory of Love*, and it is the thread we will follow in this chapter.

Margaret Hannay suggests that Lewis's point in *The Allegory of Love* was to refute five misunderstandings of Spenser current in literary circles. These are an overemphasis on political allusions, language, the allegorical nature of the work, Protestantism, and moralism. While Lewis does discuss these matters, they are not the point of his book, and such clarifications would not have established his reputation as a literary historian the way *The Allegory of Love*, in fact, did. A closer read, with an eye toward grasping the overall reach and flow of what Lewis posited, can be found in literary scholar Stephen Yandell's essay on the text. He observes that Lewis's point, building to a crescendo throughout the medieval courtly tradition, is, for Spenser "to employ the allegorical form masterfully as a way of showing the inner complexities associated with passionate, Christian, married love."[12]

The thesis of *The Allegory of Love* sets forth how the Christian concept of marriage was elevated gradually and idealized through the romantic literature of the Middle Ages. What Lewis says may have significant application in light of some of the current challenges to marriage confronting our culture today; however, applications to current circumstances will have to be drawn inferentially. Certainly, Lewis could not have anticipated the state of affairs surrounding the present interest in same-sex attraction. Nothing in the history of thought and culture could have allowed him to expect such a thing.

The absence of comment by Lewis about same-sex attraction does not mean that he was unaware of challenges that faced traditional marriage in the past. In fact, the frequency with which

---

12   Stephen Yandell, "*The Allegory of Love* and *The Discarded Image*: C. S. Lewis as Medievalist" in *C. S. Lewis: Life, Works, and Legacy. Volume 4: Scholar, Teacher, and Public Intellectual*, Bruce Edwards, ed. (Westport, CT: Prager, 2007), 126.

he writes about marriage provides much grist for thought. Most prominently, Lewis detects one particular challenge to marriage as evidenced in the Middle Ages. It was the age of the Crusades and chivalry, an age characterized by the idealization of knights in their armor, quests, and the need to rescue damsels in distress. In this time, marriage was threatened most of all by adultery.

Medieval Allegory and Courtly Love

As Lewis begins his exploration of the medieval allegory, he writes that "Humanity does not pass through phases as a train passes through stations: being alive, it has the privilege of always moving yet never leaving anything behind. Whatever we have been, in some sort we are still."[13] Elsewhere, he adds, "But surely arrested development consists not in refusing to lose old things but in failing to add new things?"[14] The maturation process demands a certain rootedness in the past with its traditions and accumulated knowledge. But, if growth is occurring, there must also be new ground explored and new horizons reached. While a new experience may provide a challenge to one's conceptual framework, nevertheless, out of this challenge, development can occur. Theology has always progressed whenever heresies occurred. These called for change in the then-held conceptual framework. This fact is supported by the history of the Church Councils. Heresies must be answered, and these answers led to more robust theology. This is no less the case in the way human thought has developed through the ages on any given topic, not the least of which is marriage. When understanding increases and progress occurs, its development is likely to be mirrored by the literature of the age.

In *The Allegory of Love* Lewis writes of continuity and change. At least two kinds of change may be observed. First, a change of

13 Lewis, *The Allegory of Love: A Study in Medieval Tradition* (New York: Oxford University Press, 1936), 1.
14 Lewis, *Of Other Worlds*, ed. Walter Hooper (New York: Harcourt, 1966), 25.

kind where the present conceptual framework has been falsified by unbending realities and the abiding paradigm must be abandoned for one better. Second, a change of degree where new data demands adjustment in currently held beliefs without the need to abandon them—a tree does not have to give up its interior rings just because it adds new ones—yet, these beliefs must be adjusted to keep up with the data. Put another way, Lewis's biggest idea, one that can be traced in all of his books, is that "reality is iconoclastic."[15]

The iconoclast breaks idols. I may have an image of God (or anything else for that matter); the new image may come after reading a book, listening to a lecture, or following a conversation. New pieces of the puzzle have come together to form a clearer image; but if I hold too tightly to the present image it will become an idol and an obstacle to growth. Lewis reminds readers that God, in his mercy, always kicks out the walls of temples we build for him because he wants to give us more of himself.[16] We want a clearer grasp of the world where we live. Even the truths we hold are subject to degrees of change. We have yet to plumb the depths of any truth we presently grasp; nor have we imagined all the possible applications of any given truth we currently know. We will never have a last word, or complete understanding of anything, but this does not mean we cannot have a sure word about some things. All truths ought to be held with this humility and honesty. This type of change, one of degree, is chronicled in *The Allegory of Love*.

Additionally, these attempts to grasp this continuity and change are destined to affect our interior life. We respond to our world not only by means of reason, but also with the heart. We are creatures of passion as well as intellect. Lewis notes that in medieval times allegory became the literary form developed to speak of and depict

15 Lewis states this concept explicitly in *A Grief Observed*, and in *Letters to Malcolm: Chiefly on Prayer*; but the idea occurs in all of his writing from his pre-Christian works up until his death.

16 Lewis, *Surprised by Joy: The Shape of My Early Life* (New York: Harcourt, Brace and Company, 1956), 165–67.

the interior life. He writes, "The inner life, and specially the life of love, religion, and spiritual adventure, has therefore always been the field of true allegory; for here there are intangibles which only allegory can fix and reticences which only allegory can overcome."[17] Lewis also observed, "The function of allegory is not to hide but to reveal, and it is properly used only for that which cannot be said, or so well said, in literal speech."[18]

The subject of courtly love filled much of the literature of the Middle Ages. It was the preoccupation of the leisured classes who had the time to write. Courtly love maintained four characteristics: humility, courtesy, the religion of love, and adultery. The fact that adultery was an idealized feature of courtly love may surprise some. However, Lewis reminds his readers that in an age where marriages were arranged, one's passions were generally focused toward someone other than one's spouse.

For instance, Lewis notes how in feudal society, marriages had nothing to do with love. "All matches were matches of interest, and worst still, of an interest that was constantly changing." Therefore, "Marriages were frequently dissolved." Furthermore, "Any idealization of sexual love, in a society where marriage is purely utilitarian, must begin by being an idealization of adultery." Lewis also notes that "according to the medieval view,

---

17 Lewis, *The Allegory of Love*, 166. While Lewis sees the importance of allegory in medieval literature, he writes much about appropriate literary form, generally, as a framework for what an author wants to say. In *A Preface to Paradise Lost* he writes that we must remember that the man who writes a love sonnet not only loves the beloved, he also loves the sonnet. In *Of Other Worlds*, he writes that sometimes fairy stories say best what needs to be said. Again, in *A Preface to Paradise Lost*, he highlights the difference between primary epic (like the works of Homer) and secondary epic (as in Virgil and Milton) as means at least as important to the authors as their matter. Furthermore, Lewis chose science fiction as a means to write romantic literature, especially that form that seeks to stir up longing for a place, ultimately for heaven. He felt he needed to go to the extraterrestrial when writing in a world where most of its farthest reaches had already been explored. Even when writing autobiography, Lewis has purposes for using that literary form as a kind of testimonial apologetic, and the form itself helps him to select, economically, what is necessary for inclusion and what is necessary to leave out. This matter of literary form for what one wants to say is something Alistair McGrath failed to realize when writing his recent biography of Lewis.

18 Lewis, *The Allegory of Love*, 166.

passionate love itself was wicked, and did not cease to be wicked if the object of it were your wife."[19] So the church taught that ardent love, even of one's spouse, was a mortal sin. And those in the Middle Ages concluded that "true love is impossible in marriage."[20] Theologians and philosophers did little to restore marriage to its proper place.

The institution of marriage was threatened by unique challenges in the Middle Ages as it is in our own day. But romantic passion came to be linked with marriage, and the story of how this occurred is the developing exposition of Lewis's *The Allegory of Love.* He says this transfer of passion to one's spouse, rather than to one's paramour, is the greatest change to occur in medieval poetry, and that "compared with this revolution the renaissance is a mere ripple on the surface of literature."[21] What is to be noted is that the transformation, as Lewis traces it, did not come from the writings of the theologians but from the poets—in fact, the Christian poets. Once again, it can be seen that artists are most often the shapers of culture, for good or for ill.

What exactly was this courtly love like? How might it be understood? For an illustration one can draw on Lewis's own explanation of that period in his life when he flirted with idealism. What he says about his own pre-conversion idealism provides a rough analogy of this "Religion of Love." After a long bout with atheism and materialism and its supporting worldview, and having seen the bankruptcy of both, Lewis turned to idealism. He writes in *Surprised by Joy* that this idealism was for him a convenience and provided a "quasi-religion." He observed it was "all *eros* . . . steaming up, but no *agape* darting down. There was nothing to fear; better still, nothing to obey."[22] This idealism which came with

19 Lewis, 13–14.
20 Lewis, 17–18.
21 Lewis, 4.
22 Lewis, *Surprised by Joy: The Shape of My Early Life* (London: Geoffrey Bles, 1955), 198.

no sense of obligation to anything truly transcendent, is analogous to the religion found in courtly love. There was religious devotion to one's beloved, but the obligations were all subjective feelings not tethered to transcendent reality.

From Courtly Love to a Christian Concept of Marriage

Lewis explains how marriage was rescued from the challenges of courtly love. To do this, he traces chronologically the gradual changes that occurred in the literature of the age and its effect on the cultural consciousness. His observations are like a stroll through the Uffizi Museum in Florence, Italy, where a careful eye can follow the gradual movement from Byzantine iconography to the more realistic, lifelike art that eventually gives way to the Romantics and Impressionists. Lewis follows the thread of the love allegory from the profligate love of the early Middle Ages to love idealized in marriage.

First, Lewis considers *The Romance of the Rose*. After the Bible and Boethius's *The Consolation of Philosophy*, Lewis says it may have been the most influential book of the Middle Ages.[23] For this present study, it is not necessary to unpack all that Lewis writes about *The Romance of the Rose*, but simply to note that it "is the story of a lover whose deepest convictions remained opposed to his love and who knew that he acted neither well nor wisely."[24] Here consciousness is awakened to conscience; the adultery that was once prized creates internal conflict. Yet, the lover's behavior remains contrary to what he knows he ought to do. The sentiment is like that of Romans 7:19, finding that we are doing what we do not want to do. How is this to be explained? Why do we rush to whatever is the immediate pleasure before us? Why do we avoid the virtue of temperance which resists the enticement of the immediate pleasure in order to gain the greater, though more remote, good? In this struggle, perhaps we find evidence that our

23 Lewis, *The Allegory of Love*, 157.
24 Lewis, 122.

wounds, accumulated in a very fallen world, are deeper than our convictions. When pleasure and convictions clash, it is convictions that are often sacrificed. Moreover, until whatever wound drives us is healed, the convictions will always suffer infirmity. What is important to notice is that the passions are directed toward someone who is not the lover's spouse and there is guilt about the matter, yet nothing is done to correct the error. In this recognition of human failure, and in the guilt that follows, Lewis chronicles a small step found in *The Romance of the Rose*, which will eventually lead to the discovery that passion can be found legitimately in marriage. Change is occurring and a thread of continuity is becoming visible.

The next text in the progression of those Lewis examines is Chaucer's *Troilus and Cressida*. He observes, "Chaucer's greatest poem is the consummation, not the abandonment, of his labors as a poet of courtly love. It is a wholly medieval poem."[25] In what way does Lewis mean "a wholly medieval poem"? Simply, that Chaucer is drawing on the romantic literature that was produced before him, using it as a source for his own material. However, Chaucer's embellishment is to take the passions described in courtly love and, though he does not turn them toward marriage *per se*, he does turn his story toward the Christian God. Again, we won't recount the story of *Troilus and Cressida*, here, but we'll say that it is the best extra-biblical story of love we have read, and we find it both tragic and moving.

For our purposes, it is important to note that although the concept of courtly love is strong in the text, and love is embodied in fornication, Chaucer begins with prayers. This connection of love and true religion is unique and noteworthy. Chaucer asks the reader to pray for him that he might tell the story of Troilus and Cressida well. Shakespeare, who borrows from Chaucer, should have also asked his readers to pray for him, as he does not tell the story nearly as well.

25 Lewis, 176.

Then Chaucer asks for more prayer. He asks for the reader's prayers on behalf of those who have never loved, that they might know love. He asks for prayers for those who have been unrequited in their love, that they might find happiness and response from their true beloved. He asks for prayers for those who have once been in love, and have now fallen out of it, that they might be restored. He asks for prayers for those who are in love that they might remain in it. This turning to heaven to understand more fully the nature of love for the beloved is unique in its time. Yet it underscores a kind of desperation one might expect when all one's hope is tethered to mere human love. It is filled with soaring expectations that are at risk of crashing disappointments due to human limitation and fallenness. Certainly, human love can be good, but it cannot replace divine love. Chaucer makes this clear.

Regarding the desperation of Troilus's situation, Lewis observes, "All men have waited with ever decreasing hope, day after day, for someone or something that does not come, and all would willingly forget the experience."[26] Chaucer's story ends with Troilus's heart desperately broken, and he is defeated on the battlefield. Then he has an out-of-body experience where his soul transcends the battlefield after his death. From this elevated perspective, he sees what must ultimately be made of all earthly loves. Chaucer then includes one last prayer: "Blessed Jesus turn all our loves to Thee."

As Lewis observes, "Chaucer, never more truly medieval and universal . . . recalls the 'yonge, fresshe folks' of his audience from human to divine love: recalls them 'hom', as he significantly says."[27] This idea, if not first encountered in Dante is, at least, developed in Dante and widely distributed through him, influencing many other authors following in his wake. For now, suffice it to say, Lewis underscores that "Chaucer has few rivals and no masters."[28]

26 Lewis, 195.
27 Lewis, 179.
28 Lewis, 197.

In his hands, this story of love and passion directs the heart to God if one ever hopes to make significant sense of human love. Passion in marriage is not yet emphasized but there is movement in a direction away from courtly love toward the management of the passions under God.

Setting the Stage for Edmund Spenser

Chaucer has set the stage for the coming of Edmund Spenser's *The Faerie Queene*, with its elevation of marriage as the place where romantic human passions ought to have their highest expression. Still, Lewis has his readers consider a few more phases in the transition from the idealization of adultery to God's ideal—in Christian marriage—as the proper place, the God-given place, to express and find fulfillment for one's earthly passions.

For example, Lewis observes that John Gower (1330–1408) is first among these transitional poets, and Lewis says Gower's significant contribution lies in his explicit concern for form and unity. The great contribution he makes to the literature of this age is to take seeming contrasts and weave them together into a coherent whole.[29] This feature in his writing resembles Christianity and how it works. If Christianity is true, and what is observed in the Scriptures is accurate, then existing tensions are often exacerbated in a fallen world. Estrangements lead to deeper estrangements and alienations proliferate unless they can be woven back together by grace. Thus, in Gower, as in Christianity, we see reconciled transcendence and immanence. Eternity can be encountered in mutability and God's sovereignty and human free will may be harmonized and reconciled. So too, concord can be found between the genders: male and female can be made into one. The universe, created by the triune God, is a place where unity and diversity can coexist. This transition step found in Gower is important in the movement from courtly love to the Spenserian reconciliation

29 Lewis, 198–99.

uniting passion and marital love with great literary success. Spenser, inheritor of all that has come before him, will rescue marriage from the challenge of courtly love and the practice of adultery. So Gower is an important link in the chain from Chaucer to Spenser.

Lewis again reminds his readers, "There are few absolute beginnings in literary history, but there is endless transformation."[30] While Lewis mentions many writers, the following will be sufficient to show that he keeps to his task. He is explaining how the literature of the Middle Ages went through incremental changes using allegory to connect passion and marriage.

The King's Quair is the next highlighted by Lewis, and of this work Lewis wrote that James I of Scotland (1394–1437) "sat down to write what most emphatically deserves to be called 'sum newe thing.'"[31] This is because James wrote of his own love for the woman who became his wife. Lewis adds that in this work one sees clearly such transition that "As the love-longing becomes more cheerful it also becomes more moral."[32] Lewis describes *The King's Quair* as the first modern book of love. Next, follows John Ludgate (c. 1371–1449) who wrote *The Temple of Glas*, in which the hero appeals to Venus that she might make a way not to "adultery but to marriage."[33] In a passage that makes the heart sink, Lewis descries the plight of young women in all times—be it in the Middle Ages, or today—who are trapped in the bondage of human trafficking, or groped by predators. Ludgate pleads on behalf of "young girls forced into marriage to mend their father's estates, and for yet younger and more deeply wronged oblates, snatched from the nursery to the cloister for the good of their father's souls."[34] This text is so contemporary. Each age has those who have drifted from a traditional view of marriage. The abusers

30 Lewis, 234.
31 Lewis, 236
32 Lewis, 242.
33 Lewis, 237.
34 Lewis, 242.

become self-referential and thereby tend toward utilitarianism. In denying the humanity of others, their own is unwittingly diminished. The abuses against conjugal fidelity have underscored the need for some kind of restoration in every age. Again, this is a reason why the path charted in *The Allegory of Love* is so important, and in some ways, so contemporary.

In William Nevill's (1497–1545) *The Castle of Pleasure*, the literary form develops into what Lewis calls "a moral allegory."[35] With Nevill, Lewis notes, "What was originally a moral necessity is becoming a structural characteristic" and "The love which he celebrates is a perfectly respectable love, ending in marriage."[36] The change is duly noted and the way is paved for Spenser's *The Faerie Queene*.

Spenser's Goal for The Fairie Queene

The Fairie Queene was written to give pleasure to Spenser's readers. Nevertheless, Lewis summarizes the author's purpose: "The goal of love which Spenser here celebrates is lawful, carnal fruition within marriage."[37] To accomplish this, Spenser utilized the influence of the Italian epic. In fact, Lewis says, "'Influence' is too weak a word for the relation which exists between the Italian epic and *The Faerie Queene*."[38] The style was best used by Ariosto

---

35 Lewis, 259.
36 Lewis, 255.
37 Lewis, *Studies in Medieval and Renaissance Literature*, "Neoplatonism in Spenser's Poetry" (Cambridge: Cambridge University Press, 1995), 149. This article was written by Lewis as a hybrid between a book review and an essay. It is as if Lewis was engaged in conversation with Robert Ellrodt's Neoplatonism in the poetry of Spenser. Ellrodt's thesis is that Spenser is not a Neoplatonist, as some have accused, due to the influence of the Cambridge Neoplatonists who held forth while Spenser was associated with that University. Lewis agrees, for the most part, with Ellrodt, and supports his argument. Lewis argues that Spenser cannot be accused of Neoplatonism, for fruition of sexual desire was "either repudiated or coldly conceded" (p. 151) by the Neoplatonists. Spenser has a far more robust view of sex and speaks of it as only properly understood in marriage; and for him this would mean a marriage between one man and one woman. To conceive of this any other way would have been unthinkable for Spenser. It is important to note that Lewis not only supports Ellrodt, but also Spenser.
38 Lewis, *The Allegory of Love*, 304.

and even more by Boiardo's *Orlando Furioso* ("The Madness of Roland") and the *Innamorato*. Supreme characteristics of this genre are "The speed, the pell-mell of episodes, the crazy carnival jollity of Boiardo [which] are his very essence."[39]

Lewis says the formula is to take any number of chivalrous romances and arrange such a series of coincidences that they interrupt one another every few pages. There is no rest. The action gives way to new and constant twists and adventure. For a popular, modern comparison, the action of an Indiana Jones movie would best capture something of the flavor. In addition, Spenser co-opts the Italian epic—a literary form already so beloved and popular in his day—for an English audience, and his readers were quick to embrace and love him. Consequently, what Spenser had to say about marriage was popularized and spread like wildfire.

Lewis observed that *The Faerie Queene* "is full of marriages."[40] These marriages are laudable, celebrated, and passionate. The image inculcated into the popular culture affected change for the good. This is the very point Lewis is making in *The Allegory of Love*. Lewis, as an academic, was gaining an ear and an eye for something of the biblical ideal. He did not compromise his craft to preach a sermon, but his careful research and convincing writing gained credit for the biblical ideal in a unique way. He realized that his scholarship could be a vehicle to help others take notice of the pleasures God intended for marriage.

Lewis took delight in this material, and elsewhere says:

> Spenser was certainly, in his own way, a religious man. And also a religious poet. But the deepest, most spontaneous, most ubiquitous devotion of that poet goes out to God, not as the One of Plotinus, not as the Calvinists' predestinator, not even as the Incarnate Redeemer, but as "the glad Creator," the fashioner of flower and forest and river, of excellent trout

39 Lewis, 300.
40 Lewis, 316.

and pike, of months and seasons, of beautiful women and "lovely knights," of love and marriage, of sun, moon, and planets, of angels, above all of light. He sees the creatures, in Charles Williams' phrase, as "illustrious with being."[41]

Lewis uses Spenser's vision of life to awaken in his readers a similar longing and desire. From here, one sees some of the Spenserian ideals manifesting themselves in a variety of ways in Lewis's other works. A few poignant examples might make the case: the awakening of love and the hope for passion between the once psychologically estranged Mark and Jane Studdock in *That Hideous Strength*, Lewis's speculation about unfallen sexuality in *A Preface to Paradise Lost*, ideas about Christian marriage expressed in *Mere Christianity*, as well as others developed in the text on *Eros* in *The Four Loves*.

On a Journey of Discovery

While this is no exhaustive study of what Lewis thought of marriage, it does take into account some significant texts from which readers might draw to discover Lewis's thoughts on the topic.

Marriage, as Lewis would see it, is by holy design. Since this is the case, where the Scriptures are unambiguous, any compromise is likely to imperil the joys and benefits of marriage as God intended them. The continuity of history regarding marriage rests in marriage as the gift of God. And human passions are best realized in marriage when God is at the center of the relationship as prescribed by Scripture. If there is design for marriage—creation implies intention—then what God had in mind for marriage must ultimately be for his glory and purpose. That which is most pleasurable for his creatures is present in the design and made malignant when divorced from the design.

---

41 Lewis, *Studies in Medieval and Renaissance Literature*, 162.

In *The Allegory of Love*, Lewis chronicled the cultural shift in attitudes whereby romantic passion found its highest expression in marriage. This account is heartening. While history seems to be a record of cultural entropy, nevertheless, in this matter of marriage, Lewis unpacked a positive change that occurred over time. Was this change for the better due to some kind of divine guidance? Was it due to human and cultural adjustment to reality? Were graces operational so that, at some level, the image of God was being restored? If this might be so, it is interesting to note that the return to a biblical ideal did not occur by means of a revival in response to fiery prophetic preaching. Rather, the continuity and change occurred slowly, over time. Literature kept the record of the cry of the human heart, longing for its ideal, embedded in its very soul since creation.

Lewis marks a change in the understanding of marriage over time: full romantic passion for another ought to be found in marriage, not outside of it. Moreover, while this has not been perfectly realized from a biblical perspective, the change that occurred in the Middle Ages was a change for the good. This historical instance should be a cause for hope no matter how things in the culture may look currently.

Lastly, Christian authors working through the fiction and poetry of the Middle Ages were the ones who rescued marriage from the threats of adultery and utility. It is important to note that a kind of cultural restoration of the dignity of marriage came from the fiction writers of the Middle Ages. It would appear that the poets did more to rescue marriage from its utility than the theologians did. If this is so, it might be advantageous to consider the use of the arts to elevate marriage once again to its biblical idealization. In fact, while one could suggest the popular arts, in their wide range of expression, have done much to assault the biblical understanding of marriage, it might require the use of the arts to once again engage the imagination to visualize the restoration of the biblical ideal. It may be possible for artists to create in a way that popular culture once again thirsts for the pleasures of an archetypal design.

Lewis takes his readers on a journey to discover the glory of God's ideal in marriage as it was traced in the developing literature of the Middle Ages. It is a journey as timely today as it was in the days of Chaucer and Spenser. In this way, Lewis as a faith-integrated Christian scholar provides an example of how sound scholarly work can function—as an apologetic for faith—speaking to the culture without preaching. In his personal life, we know that Lewis held marriage in high regard without neglecting the truth that even the best of marriages can have their ups and downs. This does not count against marriage; it only means that those who would make the best approximations to a good marriage must do so with eyes wide open. For example, in *The Horse and His Boy*, Shasta (Prince Cor) and Aravis argue throughout their adventure. And Lewis concludes the story realistically:

> Aravis also had many quarrels (and, I'm afraid even fights) with Cor, but they always made it up again: so that years later, when they were grown up, they were so used to quarrelling and making it up again that they got married so as to go on doing it more conveniently.[42]

---

42   Lewis, *The Horse and His Boy* (London: Geoffrey Bles, 1961), 199.

Magdalene College, Cambridge, where Lewis was encouraging
chaplains of the R.A.F. in their ministries to the airmen.

Public Domain image.

Chapter 2

Civil Debate in an Age of Polarity

The Personal Heresy

The Personal Heresy is a debate between C. S. Lewis and E. M. W. Tillyard, who was the Master of Jesus College at Cambridge University. Both were interested in Milton's *Paradise Lost*. Tillyard had already published a critical work on Milton. Lewis's book *A Preface to Paradise Lost* was still to come. Lewis took issue with an underlying assumption Tillyard made, that is, that Milton's *Paradise Lost* was primarily about the state of the author's mind when he wrote the book.

Lewis disagreed and wrote a critical essay in opposition, publishing it in *Essays and Studies*, a literary journal. The following year, Tillyard responded in the same journal. The next year, Lewis responded again to Tillyard. The fact that the debate was recognized as worthy of note to occupy space in three successive years of journal publications is no small matter.

And, the debate was intriguing enough that Tillyard and Lewis decided to continue it, each responding to the other, until a book could be published containing the entire conversation. *The Personal Heresy* is of great significance for all who are interested in Milton. Even more, it is significant for all who are interested in learning the art of thinking through a matter where understanding can be honed and sharpened by positive engagement with others with whom we might disagree.

Behind Lewis's Challenge to Tillyard

Lewis possessed certain assumptions that drove his challenge to Tillyard's work. Lewis was an objectivist, which means he believed that there are *knowers* (or subjects) capable of knowing. Furthermore, there are knowable objects (material objects, or objects of thought set apart by definition and developed in an inferentially coherent way). He does not deny the importance of a subject in the quest to understand, but for understanding to occur properly, the object at hand is paramount. Truth is not reality; truth is what one thinks about reality when thinking accurately about it. The object provides a necessary plumb line by which the subjective assessment might be measured and affirmed or by which assertions might be falsified. Without respect for objects—either material or conceptual—subjective judgments become anarchistic. In such cases, one is reduced to what Lewis called *subjectivism*. This occurs when the self projects onto the world, seeking to shape reality to fit its whims and predilections, rather than respond to reality with all of its complexity.

Lewis believed objectivity was possible through accurate responses to reality in matters of reason, emotion, and volition. A proper response is just only when it renders to reality its due. In cases of literary analysis, one must provide a proper response to the text if a judgment is to have merit. Due to the limits of human perception, a collective assessment of a literary text has the potential to increase the level of discovery. The give and take of debate—properly engaged, with a constant appeal to a text—could bring greater clarity and a more nuanced assessment. This was the context behind Lewis's challenge to Tillyard.

The Essence of the Debate

We come now to Tillyard's work on *Milton*, and what specifically led Lewis to enter into the debate as it is preserved in *The Personal Heresy*. As we've said, Tillyard wrote that *Paradise Lost* was about the state of Milton's mind at the time he wrote the poem.[43] Lewis said that Milton's work was actually about the content of the story Milton wanted to tell. It was a story about creation, the nature and fall of man, and the story of redemption. Therefore, it was not at all about the state of the author's mind.[44] Lewis argued that an attempt to analyze the author's mind would be an exercise in unverifiable judgments. It would likely amount to nothing more than the critic's own projection onto the author, rather than an analysis of the text itself. Such criticism of the author's mind, which is not present, removes the discussion away from the text, which *is* present. Attention is diverted from the objective and directed toward the hypothetical. Lewis asserts that criticism must be about texts themselves if a critic's judgment is ever to be validated or rendered invalid. The work is the necessary object.

---

43   E. M. W. Tillyard, *Milton* (London: Chatto & Windus, 1930). Tillyard actually wrote: "No one reading through *Paradise Lost* with any degree of seriousness can help asking with what the poem as a whole is most truly concerned, what were the feelings and ideas that dominated Milton's mind when he wrote it." (1). Later, Tillyard wrote, "It is strange how little, till quite recently, critics have concerned themselves with the meaning of *Paradise Lost*. The style, the versification, the celestial geography, the thought, who is the hero: all these have concerned the critics far more than what the poem is really about, the true state of Milton's mind when he wrote it." (201). Both quotes above are taken from the Peregrine Books edition, 1966. Lewis's remarks come from *The Personal Heresy* (New York: Oxford University Press, 1939), and can be found on p. 2.

44   *Essays and Studies: by Members of The English Association*, "The Personal Heresy in Criticism," Volume XIX, collected by D. Nichol Smith (Oxford: Clarendon Press, 1934), 7–28.

Lewis's essay was published in 1934, making it one of his earliest public presentations of critical judgment (only three years after his conversion and two years before the publication of *The Allegory of Love*).

The Content of Lewis's Argument

Lewis challenges Tillyard's claim that Milton's *Paradise Lost* "is really about, the true state of Milton's mind when he wrote it."[45] Lewis calls this approach *The Personal Heresy*, because, as has been mentioned, it takes the reader's attention away from the text itself to focus on the author. That approach is a distraction. Lewis sets forth six reasons why he rejects Tillyard's claim.

1. TO DESCRIBE EMOTION IS TO HAVE GOTTEN BEYOND THE EMOTION

Lewis begins to make his case, citing reasons why a text does not provide access to the state of the author's mind when he wrote it. For instance, when an author describes a state of emotion, is the author in that state, or removed from such a state and now considering that state of mind by recollection? Lewis would later develop these ideas in his essay "Meditation in a Toolshed"[46] and in *Surprised by Joy* where he comments about Samuel Alexander's *Space, Time, and Deity*.[47] He makes the distinction between "enjoying" or experiencing and "contemplating" or thinking about. Here in *The Personal Heresy* we have perhaps the earliest expression of Lewis's use of this distinction. "The character presented is that of a man in the grip of this emotion: the real poet is a man who has already escaped from that emotion sufficiently to see it objectively."[48] Therefore, the emotion does not express the state of the author's mind as he writes.

45   E. M. W. Tillyard and C. S. Lewis, *The Personal Heresy: A Controversy* (New York: Oxford University Press, 1939), 2.

46   Lewis, *Undeceptions*, "Meditation in a Toolshed" (London: Geoffrey Bles, 1971), 171–74.

47   Lewis, *Surprised by Joy*, 205–7.

48   Lewis and Tillyard, *The Personal Heresy*, 9.

2. *THE LITERARY CRITIQUE NECESSARY FOR DRAMA*

As an example, Lewis argues that any kind of sound, critical judgment about theatrical authorship would be threatened by Tillyard's approach. Theater requires that several points of view be on display. Each character must have a point of view. "The Drama is, in fact, the strongest witness for my contention . . . for there the poet is manifestly out of sight, and we attend not to him but to his creation."[49] Lewis asserts:

> Let it be granted that I do approach the poet; at least I do it by sharing his consciousness, not by studying it. I look with his eyes, not at him. He for the moment will be precisely what I do not see; for you can see any eyes rather than the pair you see with, and if you want to examine your own glasses you must take them off your own nose. The poet is not a man who asks me to look at *him*; he is a man who says 'look at that' and points; the more I follow the pointing of his finger the less I can possibly see of *him*.[50]

Then, he adds: "To see things as the poet sees them I must share his consciousness and not attend to it; I must look where he looks and not turn round to face him; I must make of him not a spectacle but a pair of spectacles: in fine, as Professor Alexander would say, I must enjoy him and not contemplate him."[51]

3. *THE PROBLEM OF TEXTS WITH MULTIPLE AUTHORS, AND OF TRANSLATIONS*

Lewis then asks about the "class of poetical experiences in which the consciousness that we share cannot possibly be attributed to any single individual." Poems such as *Beowulf* come immediately

---

49   Lewis and Tillyard, 8. Here also is a first use of ideas that meet the reader often enough in Lewis. See "The Seeing Eye" and the "Hamlet and Shakespeare" analogy used in *Surprised by Joy*.

50   Lewis and Tillyard, 11. This is a point Lewis will further develop in his essay "Transposition."

51   Lewis and Tillyard, 13, 99.

to mind. The reader has no knowledge of who the author is, or if the text was redacted and several authors were involved in its production. Nevertheless, the story can still be enjoyed because the text is objective. As another case in point, Lewis suggests the biblical text of *Isaiah* where he claims we do not know the author. There could have been multiple authors and redactors.[52] Lewis tips his hand, suggesting that as a young convert to Christianity he has been influenced by higher critical approaches to Scripture. This is a view he will later modify substantively, as evidenced by his late essay "Modern Theology and Biblical Criticism."[53] Lewis uses this example to make his case that criticism must be about texts and not authors. Furthermore, this problem is exacerbated when it comes to translations of texts. Whose consciousness is manifest in the translation? Is it the author's, or the translator's, or both?[54]

4. THE PROBLEM OF THE "SHARED IMAGINATION"

Lewis presses his literary attack against Tillyard by means of what he calls the *shared imagination*. "It is his business, starting from his own consciousness; whatever that may happen to be, to find that arrangement of public experiences, embodied in words, which will admit him (and incidentally us) to a new mode of consciousness."[55] Sound rhetorical theory is audience-centered; it seeks to describe reality in a way that one's audience comes to see and to be persuaded by the author's argument. To do this well the author should know something of the hearer's point of view. He or she appeals to experiences and values that are *shared* between them and draws on these to make a point. "The common world with its nights, its oaks, and its stars, which we have all seen, and which mean at least something the same to all of us, is the bank

52   Lewis and Tillyard, 12–13.
53   Lewis, *Christian Reflections*, "Modern Theology and Biblical Criticism" (Grand Rapids, MI: Eerdmans, 1967), 152–66.
54   Lewis and Tillyard, *The Personal Heresy*, 14–15.
55   Lewis and Tillyard, 26.

on which he [the author] draws his checks."[56] An appeal is made by means of these common experiences. Then the author, utilizing these shared experiences, seeks to go beyond what was previously known by author or reader. This could hardly be an expression solely of the state of the author's own mind.

5. THE AUTHOR'S ROLE AS A WINDOW

Lewis suggests that the author's role is a window through which the reader sees the world depicted in the story.[57] "A poet does what no one else can do: what, perhaps, no other poet can do; but he does not express his personality. His own personality is his starting point, and his limitation: it is analogous to the position of a window" and, as Lewis reminds his readers, "windows are not put there that you may study windows; rather that you might forget windows. And if you find that you are forced to attend to the glass rather than the landscape, then either the window or your eye is faulty."[58] One looks through the window to see beyond it into the garden. Similarly, one looks through the author's eyes to see the story depicted. It is the story to which the reader ought to attend, not to the author.

6. THE PROBLEM OF EMBELLISHMENTS

Here's another objection Lewis has to Tillyard's position. An author often "proceeds . . . partly by following the tradition of his predecessors, but very largely by the method of trial and error; and the result, when it comes, is for him, no less than for us, an acquisition, a voyage beyond the limits of his personal point of view, an annihilation of the brute fact of his own particular psychology rather than its assertion."[59]

---

56   Lewis and Tillyard, 19.
57   Lewis and Tillyard, 26–30.
58   Lewis and Tillyard, 26.
59   Lewis and Tillyard, 26-27.

For Lewis, literary embellishments occur when an author builds his story on stories that came before. How should one distinguish between an author's voice and the voices of those from which the author has drawn? For example, in Shakespeare's *Troilus and Cressida*, how would one distinguish between Shakespeare and Homer's *Odyssey* from which Shakespeare borrowed? Or Virgil's, when he wrote the *Aeneid*? Or Boccaccio's when he wrote *The Decameron*? This point is made over and over in Lewis's work on the nature of embellishments—see *The Discarded Image*,[60] "The Genesis of a Medieval Book" and "Imagination and Thought in the Middle Ages," both in *Studies in Medieval and Renaissance Literature*;[61] and in "What Chaucer Really did with *Il Filostrato*" from *Selected Literary Essays*.[62]

Conclusion of Lewis's First Objection to Tillyard

Lewis acknowledges that both Gnostic and materialist approaches to literature are destined to be faulty. The Gnostic (or hyper-spiritual) approach to literature seeks a meaning that is most likely a projection; the author paints a "Thus saith the Lord" across his or her opinions, making the projection equal to the word of God. Who could ever argue against someone who is convinced his ideas are equivalent to the word of God?

Also, Lewis believed, that "the typical modern critic is usually a half-hearted materialist." The materialist "thinks that everything except the buzzing electrons is subjective fancy . . . because outside the poet's head there is nothing but the interplay of blind forces. But he forgets that if materialism is true, there is nothing else inside the poet's head either . . . there is no foothold left for the personal heresy."[63] He adds, "You cannot have it both ways. If the universe

---

60 Lewis, *The Discarded Image: An Introduction to Medieval and Renaissance Literature* (New York: Cambridge University Press, 1964), 10–12.

61 Lewis, *Studies in Medieval & Renaissance Literature*, "The Genesis of a Medieval Book" and "Imagination and Thought in the Middle Ages" (New York: Cambridge University Press, 1966), 18–63.

62 Lewis, *Selected Literary Essays*, "What Chaucer Really did with *Il Filostrato*" (New York: Cambridge University Press, 1979), 27–44.

63 Lewis and Tillyard, *The Personal Heresy*, 28–29.

is meaningless, then so are we; if we mean something, we do not mean alone. Embrace either alternative, and you are free of the personal heresy."[64]

Tillyard's Response

In any argument, to define one's terms is wise. It removes ambiguity and the risk of equivocation. In responding to Lewis, Tillyard does this very thing. He defines his use of words such as "personal" and "personality" to add clarity to his side of the debate.[65] Then Tillyard says that "Mr. Lewis implies that 'personal' as a critical term includes every accident however trivial connected with the author. No one can complain that he does so, but I should guess that not a few supporters of the 'personal heresy' would simply ignore such trivialities in their conception of personality. They would attach them to the sphere of literary gossip, not to that of criticism."[66]

Here Tillyard does not represent Lewis fairly. He presents a *straw man* argument, trivializes Lewis's point, and then dismisses it. Certainly, it is not always easy to accurately represent an opponent in a debate. As Lewis's friend and fellow Inkling Charles Williams observed, "Not one mind in a thousand can be trusted to state accurately what its opponent says, much less what he thinks."[67] Tillyard continues, "Of course Mr. Lewis does not confine 'personal' to the trivial or accidental sense. He grants that it is possible through poetry to come into contact with a poet's temperament in the most intimate way. The reader shares the poet's consciousness."[68] Tillyard turns Lewis's words around, suggesting that Lewis grants Tillyard's point when this has not been the case at all.

---

64 Lewis and Tillyard, 30.
65 Lewis and Tillyard, 32 ff.
66 Lewis and Tillyard, 33.
67 Charles Williams, *The Descent of the Dove: A Short History of the Holy Spirit* (Grand Rapids, MI: Eerdmans, 1974), 112.
68 Lewis and Tillyard, *The Personal Heresy*, 34.

Concerned that terms such as *personal* and *personality* ought to be properly defined, Tillyard then introduces the term "normal personality" and suggests a definition that can only be construed as ambiguous. He writes that "by personality or normal personality I do not mean practical or everyday personality, I mean rather some mental pattern which makes Keats Keats and not Mr. Smith or Mr. Jones." What Tillyard means by *practical everyday personality* is not made clear so as to distinguish it either from "normal" or that "which makes Keats Keats." He further muddies the waters by saying of Keats that his is "a remarkable personality." And in a failed attempt to clarify further he adds that Keats is "someone whose personality impresses us." By what standard does Tillyard judge that a personality is remarkable or impressive, or distinguishable from "normal"? Tillyard seeks to press his defense. He argues that an author's style points to "the function of personality in poetry" and argues that "'style' readily suggests the mental pattern of the author, the personality realized in words."[69]

Here it appears a point is scored for Tillyard's side—until he presses the point too far and the argument unravels. He seeks to apply this as a defense against what Lewis wrote about translations, where multiple authors, styles, and personalities may be represented in the text. Tillyard compares translators to artists whose paintings or sculptures are attempts to "translate" some original to canvas or marble. He suggests something of the author's personality is not merely preserved, but is the only thing worth critical analysis. At this point, the reader begins to think Tillyard would be better served if he yielded rather than continued to defend what looks to be indefensible. Literary style does distinguish one author or artist from another. This is a fact in evidence when comparing texts or works of art with others. Tillyard's case is not made because the work of art is not merely reflective of the personality of the artist. Tillyard seeks to make a definitive statement—the text is the

69 Lewis and Tillyard, 35.

expression of the writer's personality—rather than an indefinite one, i.e., that *a* writer's personality may be perceived in the style of the work.

For example, one could look at several Alphonse Mucha paintings, and, seeing a new work of art, guess that it is a Mucha because it looks similar to other works he has done. But the conclusion may not be reliable. One may certainly see stylistic DNA in Mucha's graphic designs, yet the style depicted in his earlier work, and that exhibited in the more mature work of his "Slav Epic," reveals a wide stylistic range. Would something like this suggest, for Tillyard, that Mucha was a man of multiple personalities? How would Tillyard identify development within a single author's personality? When applied this way, Tillyard's argument evaporates. Neither the artist's nor the author's personality may be accurately in view. It appears Lewis's concern for the text itself is far more substantive than judgments made in an attempt to assess the author's personality, thereby avoiding the objective text itself.

From this point on, Tillyard's arguments unravel into further ambiguities. In *Mere Christianity* Lewis argues that you cannot fix an error in math by pressing on. You must go back to where the error first occurred and fix it if you ever hope to move forward accurately.[70]

Lewis's Second Argument

Lewis begins his second argument by listing each of Tillyard's objections and responding to them one at a time. Lewis appreciates the debate, adding that "In such matters to find an opponent is almost to find a friend; and I have to thank you heartily for your kind and candid contribution to the problem."[71] Again, as is true with both the disputants, there are no dismissive *ad hominems.*

70 Lewis, *Mere Christianity* (London: Geoffrey Bles, 1953), 22.
71 Lewis and Tillyard, *The Personal Heresy*, 49.

Both are respectful, and in this regard model the best in academic dialogue.

Lewis argues that a poem cannot be about the personality of the poet. When we read a poem, we are able to enter into emotional responses that would hopefully never occur when we meet a real person. For example, we may laugh at the misfortunes of the buffoon in a poem, but it would be cruel work to make fun of any of God's real creatures we might meet in real life. The poet does not meet us in his work as a real personality. Again, he focuses our attention on an imagined world of characters that may illicit from us all kinds of responses appropriate to the given situations of that imagined world, but that would be utterly inappropriate should we see someone enduring them in the world of our senses.[72]

Inviting further debate, Lewis says to Tillyard, "We have both learnt our dialectic in the rough academic arena where knocks that would frighten the London literary coteries are given and taken in good part; and even where you may think me sometimes too pert you will not suspect me of malice. If you honor me with a reply it will be in kind; and then, God defend the right!"[73]

Tillyard responds by saying, "[I]t is clear to me that our positions are beginning to approximate and that controversy has been fulfilling one of its proper functions: that of clearing away misconceptions."[74] Then he concedes several points, pleading guilty to vagueness.[75] Following this, he writes, "But I do not surrender what I had in mind, however imperfectly put on paper, to the formidable battery of Mr. Lewis's dialect. To this uniqueness I will turn, but not before thanking Mr. Lewis for his keen probings, some of which have revealed what was unsound, others helped me to mend my thoughts."[76] This is a good model of what sound

---

72 Lewis and Tillyard, 59–66.
73 Lewis and Tillyard, 69.
74 Lewis and Tillyard, 70.
75 Lewis and Tillyard, 71–73.
76 Lewis and Tillyard, 73.

debate should do for us: create in us a willingness to concede where it is necessary and clarify when we think the concession is not merited. Then Tillyard presses his earlier point that the uniqueness of style is evidence that the poet's work is ultimately about the poet's personality.

Tillyard suggests that where a literary judgment lacks good reason, we may hold to our course because other matters (emotional, cultural, psychological) affect us, and when this is the case, then certainly we must say that the poet's personality is coming through.[77] Now Tillyard seems to be seeking a concession from Lewis: not that Milton's poem is about the state of the author's mind when he wrote it, but that certainly something of the author's personality is in evidence. To this point, I doubt whether anyone would disagree that some characteristics of the creator may be in evidence in his or her creation; but the point from which Tillyard started was that this was all the poem was really about; now he appears to be looking for anything to rescue the slightest vestiges of his original argument.

Lewis scholarship owes Tillyard a great debt. He observes that Lewis has said much about what literature is not. He then demands that Lewis say what literature should express. This may be the most valuable contribution Tillyard has to make. It forces Lewis's hand and leads him to explain his views of literary critical studies with greater clarity.

Lewis's Third Argument

Lewis begins this chapter by noting, "In his last essay Dr. Tillyard is kind enough to express a hope that our controversy is gradually bringing us into agreement. In certain respects I think it is; and even where agreement may not be possible, the grounds of disagreement are being made clearer."[78] Then Lewis accepts

77 Lewis and Tillyard, 76–77.
78 Lewis and Tillyard, 95.

Tillyard's challenge to give an explanation of what poetry should be about if it is not an expression of the poet's mind at the time of his writing.

THE POET SEEKS TO DESCRIBE SOMETHING OF THE OBJECTIVE WORLD

Before Lewis outlines his theory of poetry, he feels it is necessary to say something about the real world from which the poet draws his inspiration. He says of the *real* world, that it has a "downright *interestingness*" which meets, or even besieges us daily whenever we are not ill, or tired, or preoccupied. Metaphysical assumptions abound in such a statement. Lewis does not want an approach to poetry that would focus attention on authors and thereby miss this *interestingness* of the real world that beckons or besieges— that is, the world that calls us to attend to something outside of ourselves, something that awakens in us a desire for that which transcends. This call is imperious and *ought* to be attended to. A good poet calls attention to the world of his or her made-up story; and, where there is success, an awakening of desire occurs in the mind and heart of the reader for that other world.[79] Consequently, he marks two types of symbols used in human speech, one found in the world of mathematics and one in poetry:

> The algebraical symbol comes naked into the world of mathematics and is clothed with value by its masters. A poetic symbol—like a Rose, for Love, in Guillaume de Lorris—comes trailing clouds of glory from the real world, clouds whose shapes and color largely determine and explain its poetic use. In an equation, x and y will do as well as a and b; but *The Romance of the Rose* could not, without loss, be re-written as *The Romance of the Onion*, and if a man did not see why, we could only send him back to the real world to study roses, onions, and love, all of them still untouched by poetry, still raw.[80]

79 Lewis and Tillyard, 96.
80 Lewis and Tillyard, 97.

The poet awakens interest in the real world and with all that beckons from behind it. One might add that Lewis thought Milton wrote from this perspective as well. Then Lewis writes, "These [Metaphysical] preliminaries are important for the theory of poetry which I am presently going to propound in answer to the challenge delivered at the end of Dr. Tillyard's essay."[81]

A THEORY OF POETRY

Lewis sets forth general principles regarding literary judgment which may then be applied to specific cases. There is always the possibility the application may fall below the standard; nevertheless, *an abuse does not nullify a proper use.* If objective judgments can be made at all, then questions about beauty can be settled. Should national parks be guarded to protect natural wonders? Should museums be built to preserve works of art for the pleasure of generations to come? If so, should we expect guiding principles might be abstracted that could prove helpful in making reasonable judgments in these matters?

There are rules to the game of reason and literary judgment, just as there are rules to a game of chess. Knowing the rules does not guarantee one wins the game. Skill and application of the rules is necessary. Lewis believes objective judgments are possible in matters of beauty and art because something objective is present before the senses. These things can be described and talked about. They are more than a mere extension of the self. One's judgment must be adjusted to reality. This adjusted understanding can appear in one's work. It can be embellished by a community, by culture, or by perspectives and angles of vision. It can be the work of embellishments made by generations revealing the enduring quality of some objects of beauty that seem to transcend time and place.

81 Lewis and Tillyard, 97.

LEWIS'S THEORY APPLIED TO LITERARY TEXTS

Since language can be used for purposes other than poetry (uses such as philosophy, commerce, science), the poet must use language in a particular way. Therefore, the skill of the poet (as the skill of any artist with regard to his or her materials) provides another objective basis of valuation. This has nothing to do with the artist's character or intention. An artisan may be well-intentioned even when his skill may be lacking. An artist with poor personal character may be brilliantly skilled. We may not like the lifestyle of the artist; but, as Lewis has made clear, the judgment is not about the artist, but the art.

So he infers that the material of the poet is language and language can be used in a variety of ways. Lewis seeks to focus attention on the particular ways language might be used by the artist. A scientist modifies language for the sake of quantification and measurement. A scientist says the temperature is below freezing. Turning to a thermometer, he "escapes from the sensuous altogether into the world of pure quantities." Meanwhile, a poet modifies common language to enable the reader to feel the very quality of the experience. A poet may use an analogy to say what it feels like to be in weather below freezing: "It felt like a slap in the face." Poetry uses its tools, "extra-logical elements of language—rhythm, vowel-music, onomatopoeia, associations," one might add metaphors, similes, and analogy, "to convey the concrete reality of experiences."[82]

While Lewis has given some basis (certainly not all) for making a certain degree of judgment regarding literary beauty and art, he wants to prevent the false notion that ambiguity in these matters can be eliminated. Reality is complex, and the apprehension of beauty should always stretch the observer who seeks to enjoy and understand it. "It is therefore not usually possible, and never necessary to say of a composition in any absolute sense 'this is

82   Lewis and Tillyard, 108.

poetry' . . . What we can say is 'this is further in the poetical direction than that,'" he writes.[83] It is the burden of the critic to explain why this is so, tethering his or her observations to what is there, that is, to the text itself.

Lewis says, "[I]n ordinary terminology, we mean by a tall man or a rich man one who is taller or richer than most, so by a poem we mean a composition which communicates more of the concrete and qualitative than our usual utterances do. A poet is a person who produces such compositions more often and more successfully than the rest of us." In one sense, all men and women are poets "in the sense that they can and do exploit the extra-logical properties of language to produce utterances of the concrete which have a value higher than zero. We do not usually call them poets: just as I am not called a carpenter though I could, at a pinch, put up some sort of shelf."[84] Lewis says that a generalization is not a thing in itself. It is an abstraction. He explains:

> In space and time there is no such thing as an organism, there are only animals and vegetables. There are no mere vegetables, only trees, flowers, turnips, etc. That there are no "trees," except beeches, elms, oaks and the rest. There is no such thing as 'an elm." There is only *this* elm, in such a year of its age at such an hour of the day, thus lighted, thus moving, thus acted on by all the past and all the present, and affording such and such experiences to me and my dog and the insect on its trunk and the man a thousand miles away who is remembering it. A real elm, in fact, can be uttered only by a poem. The sort of things we meet in poetry are the only sort we meet in life—things unique, individual, lovely, or hateful. Unfortunately, however, poetry does not, as poetry, tell us whether the particular ones she describes do, in fact exist.

83 Lewis and Tillyard, 108.
84 Lewis and Tillyard, 108–9.

Lewis continues, "Only science can tell you where and when you are likely to meet an elm: only poetry can tell you what meeting an elm is like. . . . We abstract to inquire whether God exists: Dante shows you what it would be like if He did."[85]

Having defined poetic language and distinguished it from abstract or scientific language, Lewis notes, "But language must be about something. You cannot just 'say.' You must say this or that."[86] The critic who only speaks of his likes and dislikes of a work tells us nothing about the work itself. Without an adequate description, a reader cannot determine if the critic's likes and dislikes have merit. "Poetry is an exploitation of language to convey the concrete." Furthermore, Lewis adds, "The means are art; the thing conveyed, said, or uttered is not. It is everybody's business."[87]

At the end of the day a good poem should have two qualities, he explains. First, the story must be interesting; that is, it should arouse interest.[88] Being interesting means that it is not a projection. In fact: "We lose ourselves not in the poet but in that wherein he is lost—in the adventure of Crusoe, the flowing of the Oxus, or the rotundity of Falstaff."[89] He writes of that form of poetry that "communicates such experiences as all men have had, so that simple readers exclaim 'How true', and classicists call it a 'just representation of general nature', and realists say that the poet is stripping off the mask of convention and facing 'the facts.'"[90] A connection has occurred between the author and reader; the point of connection is the real, objective world where both live. The author has appealed to the shared experience and met the reader on common ground, awakening something in the heart of the reader.

The second quality is seen in the nature of this arousal. These interesting features, Lewis says, "should have a desirable permanent

85 Lewis and Tillyard, 110.
86 Lewis and Tillyard, 111–12.
87 Lewis and Tillyard, 114.
88 Lewis and Tillyard, 96, 116, 119, 120, 121.
89 Lewis and Tillyard, 100.
90 Lewis and Tillyard, 102.

effect on us if possible—it should make us either happier, or wiser, or better."[91] He observes, "It is the message not the messenger that has my heart."[92] He makes the point once again that the poem is not about the state of the author's mind when he wrote; something much more significant is there. This drives Lewis's worldview and his views about literature again and again, as we saw in the first chapter, views that are always faith-integrated. Nature should awaken desire, and when the poet writes well, he or she becomes a servant of a wooing God, whether or not the poet is aware that this is so. It is not an act of manipulation. Rather, it is an act of speaking the truth either clearly or hiddenly (sometimes God himself hides) with power to describe reality well. And in that act the poet awakens desire in the reader and sends him in quest of the transcendent: the metaphysical reality behind all phenomena.

Final Observations

In *The Personal Heresy*, Lewis calls for criticism of texts and urges critics to avoid other distractions. Criticism is not about the personality of an author; it is about what the author has written. We hardly know ourselves and we are often blind to our own motives. How can we be confident that we have understood the motives and intentions of others? An author is seldom proximate to the literary critic. Consequently, when we turn from the analysis of the text to the analysis of the author's personality, could it be little more than projection? We see pictures in the flickering fire and stories in the clouds and constellations that are not really there. Lewis advises in this book that critics would do well to stick to the objectivity of texts. Judgments are supported or refuted by what is actually in the text itself. The accuracy and reliability of the critic's judgments can be checked. Lewis writes to urge critics to steer a course away from what he calls subjectivism.

91   Lewis and Tillyard, 120.
92   Lewis and Tillyard, 103.

All who want an example of serious, respectful academic dialogue without rancor should read this book. The Lewis/Tillyard debate produces light, not heat. Understanding is benefitted. Both authors are capable of making points and conceding points, for both demonstrate a level of security and confidence in their field.

Because neither Lewis's nor Tillyard's ideas are themselves last words about beauty and art, it follows that dialogue to advance understanding must be encouraged. In fact, Lewis invited engagement since he was constantly open to revising and refining his grasp of virtually everything he studied. He appreciated the benefits of conversation in these matters and had respect for the perspectives of others. When challenged, however, he rightly expected that the challenge be validated objectively. This was vividly attested to when once, in a debate with a relativist, Lewis's objectivism was challenged. "How do you know there isn't a blue cow on that piano right now?" asked the relativist. Lewis responded, "In what sense blue?"[93] Without an appeal to an object the suggestion blue is meaningless. So too, "Beautiful!" or, "This is great art!" have no meaning without an appeal to objective reality. The idea that beauty, or great art, is merely arbitrary is equally false. The claim that beauty is objective does not solve all problems. Demonstrating in what way the beauty exists or establishing the claim that the art ought to be appreciated is far more difficult.

---

93   Erik Routley, *C. S. Lewis at the Breakfast Table*, "A Prophet," James Como, ed. (New York: Macmillan, 1979), 35.

Chapter 3

A Book Born in Friendship

Arthurian Torso

Arthurian Torso is generally neglected by readers familiar with Lewis's popular works. Yet it sheds light on his interest in the Arthurian legend, a work essential to medieval scholarship, and it gives vocabulary and sense to the robust theology of Lewis's friend and fellow Inkling Charles Williams. Therefore, as a door to the rich theology of Williams, *Arthurian Torso* allows the reader to think more deeply about God and the world he has made. Lewis is an informed and helpful guide through this material.

Lewis and Williams met in a unique way. Lewis read *The Place of the Lion*;

Williams read *The Allegory of Love*. They wrote letters of praise to one another, and the letters, according to Lewis, crossed in the mail. Consequently, Lewis went to London to meet Williams, and their friendship began. Not long after, when the bombing of London began during World War II, the Oxford University Press, for whom Williams worked as an editor, moved its London operations to Oxford. Lewis immediately invited Williams to join the Inklings, the literary group composed of such authors as J. R. R. Tolkien, the Chaucer scholar Neville Coghill, eighteenth-century literary critic Lord David Cecil, Lewis's brother and French historian Major Warren Lewis, philosopher Austin Farrar, literary critic Hugo Dyson, and others. They read aloud from books they were writing and benefitted from the criticism and response of their colleagues. In fact, Lewis dedicated his first popular work in Christian apologetics, *The Problem of Pain*, to the Inklings. Williams fit right in and became one of the Inklings' most significant members.

As World War II ended, Oxford University Press reopened its offices in London. Since Williams would be leaving Oxford to return home, Lewis organized the Inklings to prepare a *festschrift* for Williams. The book was published as *Essays Presented to Charles Williams*[94] and was edited and introduced by Lewis. It is significant since it represents what might be the only collaborative work by the Inklings. It is also the first place Tolkien published his now-famous essay "On Fairy-Stories." This gives evidence of Lewis's appreciation for Williams and the degree to which he valued his friendship.

Unfortunately, Williams died unexpectedly in May of 1945. He left behind a series of poems retelling the Arthurian legends through the eyes of Taliessin, the poet at King Arthur's court. Two books were published—*Taliessin through Logres* and *Region of the Summer Stars*—neither of which garnered much attention, partly

---

94   C. S. Lewis, ed., *Essays Presented to Charles Williams* (Grand Rapids, MI: Eerdmans, 1966).

because the symbolism was too personal to Williams and, for the uninformed reader, too cryptic. A debt of friendship led Lewis to write a work of literary introduction and criticism of the Williams material. Since Williams discussed the poetry and its imagery with Lewis and Tolkien, Lewis was familiar with Williams's intentions for the work. The thought behind the poetry, as well as the theological insight it contains, is profound; but without a proper guide, it remains abstruse to the average reader. Lewis, aware of the significance, wanted to make Williams's ideas more accessible to wider audiences.

After careful synthesis of the poems, Lewis gave a series of lectures about the poetry at Oxford in the autumn of 1945. As Dante needed a Virgil to guide him through the *Inferno* so Williams required Lewis's instincts and insights in order to grasp the concepts embedded in his work. Later, in 1948, these lectures were published as *Arthurian Torso*: *Containing the Posthumous Fragment of "The Figure of Arthur" by Charles Williams and a Commentary on the Arthurian Poems of Charles Williams by C. S. Lewis.*[95]

One may wonder why Williams chose the Arthurian story as a way to communicate theological insight. For Williams, as well as for any faith-integrated person, every subject becomes a segue for theological reflection. In a world made by God, and inhabited by God, attention to his imperious call on our lives can come from any quarter. The Arthurian stories seemed to Williams an adequate means to bear the weight of theological ideas. Lewis thought the same. He took the complex thought of Williams and made its wisdom and insight more accessible.

---

95 Lewis, *Arthurian Torso: Containing the Posthumous Fragment "The Figure of Arthur" by Charles Williams and a Commentary on the Arthurian Poems of Charles Williams by C. S. Lewis* (New York: Oxford University Press,1948). The book was later republished as *Taliessin Through Logres, The Region of the Summer Stars, Arthurian Torso, by Charles Williams with an Introduction and Commentary by Lewis* (Eerdmans, 1974).

The Figure of Arthur

Lewis begins *Arthurian Torso* by including the prose piece *The Figure of Arthur*. This was written by Williams and, although never published during Williams's lifetime, had been read aloud and discussed at an Inklings gathering. Williams gives a historical recounting of how certain elements entered into the legend over the centuries. Lewis wrote that one characteristic of medieval literature was the idea of embellishment. The old stories, told and retold, were enjoyed and cherished. Each retelling would add new elements to the story. So grew the legend (or myth) of King Arthur and his court. Tolkien called this kind of embellished story "the Cauldron of Story."[96]

Many of us heard in elementary school the story of *Stone Soup*. In days long gone by, it was the law of the land that local villages would billet soldiers returning from the wars as they were wearily traveling home. Often, the townspeople saw this as an inconvenience, and seeing from a distance soldiers coming their way, would pack up the village square, retreat into their homes, and close the doors and shutters. When the soldiers of the stone soup tale arrived at such a village they were well aware of what was occurring. One soldier would call out to another that he was hungry and hoped his companion would once again make the stone soup that they had so enjoyed the night before. The curiosity of the village people peeking through their shutters was aroused. The soldiers filled a large kettle with water from the river. Then a soldier reached into his pocket, retrieved a velvet envelope, and out of it withdrew a smooth, round stone. He held it to his nose and seemed to breathe in the aroma. The villagers cracked their shutters wider, eager to see more clearly what the soldiers were doing. The stone was dropped into the kettle and each man bent

---

96 J. R. R. Tolkien, *Essays Presented to Charles Williams*, "On Fairy Stories," C. S. Lewis, ed. (New York: Oxford University Press, 1947), 49, 53.

toward the pot to watch. "I can almost taste it now," one soldier said. Another responded, "Yes, but it is too bad we do not have onions as we did last night." At that moment, curiosity prompting him, a villager popped open his shutters and called out, "I've got onions!" He rushed down and cut up the onions, added them to the soup, and stood with the others staring into the pot. Another soldier said, "If only we had carrots," to which another villager opened his shutters and said, "I've got carrots!" This pattern continued until the pot was full of meats, vegetables, spices, and other savory delights. All the villagers were now present. Lanterns were hung, village musicians started to play, and all ate. When it came time to provide sleeping quarters for the soldiers, the townspeople fought over who had the privilege of hosting them. This is the way of story; each generation takes from things past and, as Lewis observed, embellishes it into something new, yet with the lingering aroma of the old. The embellishments often echo cultural developments as well.

In *The Figure of Arthur*, Williams gives a historical account of how the legend came to be and how it grew. The addition of the Grail and the introduction of Christianity brought a kind of unity to the various elements of the Arthur story.[97] This development occurred at the very time the doctrine of the Eucharist and the rituals associated with it were also developing.[98] The idea of the Grail linked theology and myth.[99] The Sacrament, for some, became the very embodiment of Christ in wine and bread. Nevertheless, Williams claims that St. Peter Damian (1007–1072) was the first to introduce the term *transubstantiation*, suggesting that the bread and wine became the actual body and blood of Christ. It was an argument against the rise of Gnosticism.[100]

97 Lewis, *Arthurian Torso*, 13.
98 For Williams's full recounting of the history of Eucharistic theological development see Lewis, *Arthurian Torso*, 13–21.
99 Lewis, *Arthurian Torso*, 16–20.
100 Lewis, *Arthurian Torso*, 14, 17–19.

In "The Coming of the King," Williams records the process whereby Arthur is eventually identified as a King and tells of the developing characteristics of his reign. In Arthur's Court "the men are all celebrated for their valour, the women for their wit. Love encourages all to virtue, the women especially to chastity, the men especially to valour. But nobility in all things thrives in them all."[101] In Williams's poem, Arthur was to be an embodiment of God's law.[102] Williams observed that it is not until *Layamon's Brut* that the matter of the round table is added to the cauldron of the developing story. At this table, law would bind all to the realm and to one another. Love among the knights encouraged chivalry and chastity. In a deeply fallen world even this could not guarantee a perfect society. There are those in Court who will offend against chastity, loyalty, and justice. Arthur's nephew Mordred cultivates the evil that is already in him, whereas Guinevere and Lancelot are well-meaning but flawed.[103]

Williams then chronicles "The Coming of Love" to Arthur's court. Here the story was embellished further by the addition of courtly love, which included "the Religion of Love" that is the devotion of the lover to the object of that love. All is done sacrificially and in homage to the one. Courtly love included courtesy, acts great or small of self-offering for the beloved, and humility, which always puts devotion to another before all else. The real power developing in the myth was the coming of love as idealized in marriage. There were dalliances and these unfortunate events led to consequences, but, as Geoffrey of Monmouth said, "love in the king's court . . . encouraged all lovers to virtue"— which meant the reservation of physical union to marriage.[104] Failures occur; therefore, as the myth developed alongside the Christian tradition, redemption would be necessary.

101   Lewis, *Arthurian Torso*, 31.
102   Lewis, *Arthurian Torso*, 41.
103   Lewis, *Arthurian Torso*, 43.
104   Lewis, *Arthurian Torso*, 55.

In "The Coming of the Grail," something more than a mere counter to Gnosticism is presented. The Grail's presence in the story embodies the Christian elements of redemption characterized by the high courtesy. In death Christ proclaimed, *I offer my life for you.* The Eucharist, of which the Grail was a sacred symbol, echoes the courtesy. Achievement of the Grail signaled hope in a fallen world. In commenting on this Lewis asks, "What then is the achievement of the Grail?" He answers, "It is Christ-consciousness instead of self-consciousness. . . . It is Christian, orthodox, and Trinitarian."[105] The Grail allows Williams to introduce his doctrine of "exchange" into the story (a topic that will be considered later).

Williams and the Arthuriad

Lewis helps by explaining Williams's unique use of terms and place names. This is of vital importance in making Williams more accessible to the reader. Each term reveals something of the development of Williams's narrative, and of the theology embedded in that narrative. There are also place names and each bears a theological concept.

LOGRES (PRONOUNCED: LOW' GRESS)

This term indicates the name of King Arthur's realm, the Britain of Arthur. The word is derived from the Welsh word *Lloegr,* "a land of fairy," which was also Britain, or, more specifically, a land within Britain.[106] Williams observes that Logres was also used to speak of "Britain in an enlarging world—Britain and more than Britain."[107] One might say it was where awareness of the operations of transcendence was not yet suppressed.

BROCELIANDE (PRONOUNCED: BRO-SEALY, AHN' DAY)

The Wood of Broceliande is west of Logres, off the western coast of Cornwall—as Lewis observes, "both a forest and a

---

105   Lewis, *Arthurian Torso,* 79.
106   Lewis, *Arthurian Torso,* 53, 99.
107   Lewis, *Arthurian Torso,* 80.

sea—a seawood." This description bears a familiar resemblance, perhaps even a partial inspiration for the floating islands of Lewis's *Perelandra*. Through Broceliande runs a road that leads to one of two destinations. The road for some leads to *Carbonek,* "the castle of Holy things, the dwelling place of Pelles the guardian of the Grail."[108] And beyond Carbonek, on the same road, to Sarras the "Land of the Trinity," or Heaven. In the Castle of Holy things, one discovers the iconography that awakens desire and sets the soul questing for the Reality that transcends the symbols. The castle stands as an "Affirmation of Images."

In the opposite direction the road through Broceliande a leads to the Antipodean Ocean. Lewis explains that the Antipodean Ocean is the realm of *P'o-lu,* or Hell. He clarifies that "Consciousness in P'o-Lu consists only of 'rudiments or relics,' 'the turmoil of the mind of sensation.' It is on the very fringe of Hell."[109] Similarly, in the hell of Lewis's *The Great Divorce,* there exists no human; it is a place only of remains, the vestiges of what was once human. In light of this, Lewis adds that for Williams, "The Fall was an alteration in knowledge."[110] Consequently, "Hell is inaccurate."[111]

Lewis's own thought about the nature of hell falls in line with Williams's. In essence, hell is an asylum, and those in the asylum deny the reality of God, who is the central fact of the universe. They act as if *they* are God. The lunacy is depicted in the words of John Milton's Satan in *Paradise Lost* that it is "better to reign in Hell than serve in Heaven."[112] For Lewis and Williams, hell is a place for the eternally incorrigible. Lewis says in *The Great Divorce,* "There are only two kinds of people in the end: those who say to God, 'Thy will be done,' and those to whom God says,

---

108   Lewis, *Arthurian Torso,* 99.
109   Lewis, *Arthurian Torso,* 100.
110   Lewis, *Arthurian Torso,* 109.
111   Lewis, *Arthurian Torso,* 106.
112   Lewis, *The Great Divorce: A Dream* (London: Geoffrey Bles, 1945), 64. Lewis takes this from the following source: John Milton, *The Complete Poetical Works of John Milton* (Boston: Houghton Mifflin, 1924), 106.

'Thy will be done.' All that are in Hell, choose it. Without that self-choice there could be no Hell."[113]

Lewis adds in *The Problem of Pain*, "I willingly believe that the damned are, in one sense, successful, rebels to the end; that the doors of Hell are locked on the *inside*."[114] This echoes Job 21:14 where those going down to Sheol "say to God, 'Depart from us! We do not even desire the knowledge of Thy ways. Who is the Almighty, that we should serve Him?'" Williams says, "Since the Fall, instead of Co-inherence there is Incoherence."[115] This is why Milton names the capital of hell Pandemonium, which literally means "all demons" and later comes to mean the place of confusion and nonsense.[116]

What is clear here is that the poetry presents sin as man playing God of his own life. This estranges humankind from God. It also estranges humans from one another. If all are playing God of their own lives, the world is inhabited by anarchists, and anarchists are unable to participate in stable community. Furthermore, sin, understood in this way, leads to estrangements within oneself. It is characterized by the separation of head from heart, soul from flesh, memory from reality—what psychologists call being *split off*. It leads to a fractured life rather than an integrated one. Sin alienates from reality whenever the moral life is compromised. Its world is artificial. Evil is rationalized away, and all who refuse to accommodate themselves to the real become victims of falsehood. Without sensitivity to reality, we have nothing objective with which to confirm or deny our notions, thoughts, or judgments. We are left with mere subjectivism and self-referentialism in our thoughts about the world, and a rationalized, utilitarian treatment of others destroys community. People matter, not objectively as having been made in the image of God; they matter if they can be used by the self-referential.

113 Lewis, *The Great Divorce*, 66–67.
114 Lewis, *The Problem of Pain* (New York: Macmillan, 1962), 127.
115 Lewis, *Arthurian Torso*, 149.
116 Milton, *The Complete Poetical Works of John Milton*, 112, 215.

In the denial of the humanity of others, one's own humanity atrophies. It is for this reason Arthur's Camelot will fracture. Lewis masterfully develops these themes in *The Great Divorce*, and in his depiction of the nefarious character Weston, whose loss of humanity earns him the title the "Unman" in *Perelandra*. Both these books by Lewis were published around the time he gave his Arthuriad lectures at Oxford (1944–45). Williams's influence on Lewis and the cross-pollination that occurred between the two are clear.

The road through Broceliande leads to either heaven or hell. Lewis says, "All journeys away from the solid earth [that is reality] are equally, at the outset, journeys into the abyss."[117] This is true as Williams depicts the Arthur story and it is certainly true of Arthur himself. He must choose the way he will go: through Broceliande, toward heaven or hell. To prepare the reader for what is at stake in Arthur's choice, Lewis sets the stage, drawing from Dante's *De Monarchia* that "Function Precedes Essence."[118] God's very acts of creation imply intention; he assigns his unique purposes to all, giving each the very essence and gifts needed to fulfill those purposes. For instance, in the creation account, God made light on day one but did not make the luminaries (the sun, moon, and stars: the essences that emit light) until day four. Dante believed God's purposes were prior to creation. Consequently, one's essence exists for the sake of an assigned purpose. One's purpose is exercised in service, and service is to be rendered on behalf of others. It is part of what Williams calls the Divine Co-inherence, the participation in the divine courtesy, which is to say, "I offer my life in service for you." In healthy community, it is always reciprocated but never coercively so. Williams calls this self-offering The Doctrine of Exchange. The service is given through acts of love.

---

117 Lewis, *Arthurian Torso*, 101.
118 Dante Alighieri, *The* De Monarchia *of Dante Alighieri*, edited with translation and notes by Aurelia Henry. (Boston and New York: Houghton, Mifflin and Company, 1904), 3.

Lewis comments that Arthur's fatal flaw occurs when he asks the question, is "the King made for the Kingdom, or the Kingdom made for the King?"[119] He has violated his God-given purpose to serve the people. Camelot unravels; the king has gone against the grain of the divine design of the universe. The Doctrine of Exchange has been ignored and the "high courtesy" violated. Camelot fractures. We see something similar in Lewis's Queen Jadis of Charn, who will become the White Witch of Narnia. Her kingdom also unravels due to her own self-referential ways. When civil war breaks out in the world of Charn where her sister reigns as Queen, she speaks "The Deplorable Word," destroying her world and saving only herself. In that moment, she becomes like Williams's Arthur. She also becomes anti-Aslan, who, by contrast, gives up his life in an expression of the high courtesy to save others. One could also add that this saving of self while destroying others is, in fact, an expression of anti-Christ.[120]

Arthur, on the path that runs through Broceliande, has taken a step toward hell. He has stepped away from the natural order of things. He has moved outside of the high courtesy by moving away from the divine purpose of his role as king. He begins to improvise. Purpose now exists for the sake of essence. The fall, which occurs here, has been "an alteration of knowledge." It turns the world upside-down. Put another way, Arthur has violated what Lewis calls the Tao or the doctrine of objective value.[121] Stepping away from objective value, he has stepped into a void of unreality. Tragically, his act does not merely affect himself. All who live in his kingdom suffer the consequences.

119 Lewis, *Arthurian Torso*, 112.
120 See Lewis's accounts in *The Magician's Nephew* and also *The Lion, the Witch and the Wardrobe*.
121 Lewis, *The Abolition of Man* (Las Vegas, NV: Lits, 2012), 16.

As Williams tells the story, Lancelot also fails when he chooses illicit love for Guinevere over his loyalty to his friend King Arthur, and he chooses against the responsibilities of his calling as a knight of the round table. It is no longer my life for you, but your life for me. So it is with Guinevere when she chooses adultery with Lancelot over her vows to the king. The major characters, even the noblest, are flawed. Both dignity and depravity can be seen in them. Therefore, Williams turns to themes of redemption.

BYZANTIUM

Lewis says that Byzantium represents the City, and for Williams the city is the place of everyday life and commerce. One works, and another pays for the work. The coinage of the city is the means of exchange and in it the high courtesy is embodied. The worker gives his life through his labor and the employer gives of himself through the offering of his coin in *exchange* for this labor. The coin enables the worker then to use it in exchange for goods. The city gives evidence to the high courtesy, and in Britain the stamp of the king (or sovereign), is pressed upon the coin and written across the entire process. This is all done under the sovereignty. Participation in the exchange gives evidence of a redemptive process. One lays down his life for another.

In the city, one observes the Co-inherence. This speaks of those who are participating in high courtesy. Participation occurs at times knowingly and sometimes unknowingly. Nevertheless, the work of the Kingdom and the work of the Emperor are occurring. In fact, redemptive processes are always occurring. Everyone is either moving toward everlasting glory or everlasting horror. On the shoulders of each of us is laid the "Weight of Glory," and each is either helping others toward the glory or the horror. This is the road through Broceliande.

Byzantium is the place where redemption is potential. In an attempt to clarify Williams's meaning, Lewis refers to Williams's

work on "The Theology of Romantic Love." He looks at the role
of Beatrice in Dante's city of Florence and the role Virgil plays as
Dante writes of romantic love. Let me provide some background for
those less familiar with Virgil's *Aeneid* or Dante's *Vita Nuova* and
The Divine Comedy. These have a significant place in Williams's
poetry and theology.

In the *Aeneid*, Aeneas, a citizen of Troy, is awakened as the
Greeks begin to sack the city. Aeneas is warned in a vision that he
must flee the burning city and establish a new one. He obeys, and
his entire adventure finds him as a man caught between the two
cities, the city of his birth and the city that will one day be. St.
Augustine, not a fan of the classical myths, was intrigued by this
one. He thought it was descriptive of all of us. We are all, to some
degree, pilgrims caught between two cities: the city of our birth
and the city that will one day be. Aeneas sets out to build Rome.
Romantic longing is rooted in this story; the longing for a place
that has yet to be. It is ultimately a heaven longing. In *A Preface to
Paradise Lost*, a book Lewis dedicated to Williams in 1942, Lewis
translates these two lines from Virgil's *Aeneid*:

> Twixt miserable longing for the present land
> And the far realms that call them by fates command.
> (Aeneid V. 656)

Then he makes the following observation: "It will be seen that in
these two lines Virgil, with no intention of allegory, has described
once for all the very quality of most human life as it is experienced
by anyone who has not yet risen to holiness or sunk into animality.
. . . In making this one legend symbolical of the destiny of Rome,
he has, willy-nilly, symbolized the destiny of Man."[122]

As Aeneas longs for Troy and for Rome, so Dante, in *Vita
Nuova* and *The Divine Comedy*, thinks he longs for Beatrice. He

122 Lewis, *A Preface to Paradise Lost*, 37–38.

eventually discovers there is something "further up and further in" that he wants far more. Lewis writes of Beatrice: "in her (at that moment) [the moment Dante meets Beatrice] Paradise is actually revealed, and in the lover Nature is renovated. The great danger is lest he should mistake the vision, which is really a starting point, for a goal; lest he should mistake the vision of paradise for arrival there."[123] If Dante embraces Beatrice as an end, rather than sees her as a means to a greater end, he will fall into the error of King Arthur, Lancelot, Guinevere, and all others who have betrayed the true treasure of God for those things that cannot last, the things moth and rust destroy.

It is Taliessin, the poet, who guides the reader through Williams's telling of the Arthurian myth, much in the same way Virgil, the poet, guides Dante through the *Inferno* and *Purgatorio*. Lewis writes: "Taliesin's voice sharpens; he is thinking of Virgil. More exactly he is thinking of . . . Palinurus [the helmsman of Aeneas's ship] who died with no more reward for all his wandering than 'Italy seen from a wave'" (*Aeneid* VI).[124] Even as Beatrice cannot replace God—no more than a gift can replace the giver of the gift— so too, even poetry, in the end, must plunge into the void. Lewis warns that poetry, Beatrice, and Arthur's Logres must all die, giving way to something greater. Lewis acknowledges that nothing in this world can fully approximate that for which the heart most yearns, adding that ours "is a universe that breathes a Universal sigh." Even Moses can never see the full glory of God and must see the promised land from a distance. Virgil was not to realize fully the effect of his own poetry. Lewis says, "He made honey not for himself; he helped to save others, himself he could not save."[125]

For Dante, Beatrice comes out of heaven to collect him and usher him to the very threshold of the vision of God. He says,

123 Lewis, *Arthurian Torso*, 116–17.
124 Lewis, *Arthurian Torso*, 120.
125 Lewis, *Arthurian Torso*, 121.

"She . . . smiled and looked at me; then turned to the eternal fountain."[126] She was a means, not an end. Her participation in the high courtesy was to offer herself as a guide. Dante, to follow well, could not be distracted. He must want something more than Beatrice, lest his road through Broceliande lead to hell rather than heaven. When Lewis's own wife, Joy Davidman, died, Lewis sought to understand what she meant to him. He wrote of his sorrow in *A Grief Observed.* In the world of exchange, had he not loved her, his heart would not break at her passing. Yet in her passing, he discovered that she could never do for him what only God could do for him. Her passing was also a gift to Lewis. He concludes *A Grief Observed* with the Italian, "She smiled, but not at me. *Poi si tornò all' eterna fontana.*"[127] To know this is to pass through Broceliande toward heaven. It is to discover in Byzantium, the city of exchange, participation in the high courtesy of heaven leading toward heaven itself. In the fallen world of Logres, the way to heaven can be found. Williams thought so, and Lewis, paying a debt of exchange to his beloved friend, wrote about it for others. This too, was an expression of the high courtesy.

It is in the city of Byzantium where the anticipation of acts of true exchange and heaven's high courtesy can be awakened and potentially rekindle the flame of true love and redemption. At Logres Lewis notes, "We are happily reminded of the complexity of the real world. Inside the growing failure of Logres something else is springing up."[128] One of the laws of the city is that "Unless devotion is given to a thing which must prove false in the end, the thing that is true cannot enter."[129]

---

126 Dante Alighieri, *The Divine Comedy of Dante Alighieri,* "Paradise" Canto XXXI, LL. 91–92., trans. Charles Eliot Norton, *The Great Books of the Western World,* Volume 21, Robert Maynard Hutchins, Editor in Chief (Chicago: Encyclopedia Britannica, 1952), 154.
127 Lewis, *A Grief Observed* (New York: HarperCollins, 1994), 76.
128 Lewis, *Arthurian Torso,* 134.
129 Lewis, *Arthurian Torso,* 135.

Further Concepts in the Arthuriad

In Williams's poetry, redemption comes in the figure of Galahad and the quest of the Grail. Lewis admits the imagery begins to bog down in complexity.

While hinting at the means of redemption, Williams presents two problems. The first is found in the image of a Bedouin shepherd who walks with a stone in one hand and a shell in the other. The image is borrowed from Wordsworth's *The Prelude*. The stone represents reason, the shell is a symbol of the romantic longings of the heart. The head and the heart are estranged from one another due to separation at the Fall. Here Lewis observes that the first problem of life is how "to fit the stone in the shell." How can the head, reason, be reconciled to the heart and the life of the emotions and deep longings?[130]

The second problem is directly related to the first. Regarding the question "Who can reconcile head and heart," a slave girl asks Taliessin: "Who knows? And who does not care?"[131] This is a play on words. The answer is found in God who knows and God who cares. At this moment, "Galahad emerges as a symbol of Christ."[132] As Galahad is central to the process of redemption in Logres, so too must everyone participate in a similar way in the high courtesy of redemption. Here, Williams's poem breathes into the literature of the Arthurian stories that which is behind every story; that is, "God was in Christ (and we might add continues to be in the Body of Christ, the Church) reconciling the world to Himself" (2 Cor. 5:18-19).

Other Theological Ideas

There are other terms in the *Arthurian Torso* Lewis underscores to emphasize the concept of reconciliation.

---

130   Lewis, *Arthurian Torso*, 168.
131   Lewis, *Arthurian Torso*, 170.
132   Lewis, *Arthurian Torso*, 178.

Lewis writes that two spiritual maxims were constantly present to the mind of Charles Williams: "This also is Thou" and "Neither is this Thou." Holding the first we see that every created thing is, in its degree, an image of God. The faithful apprehension of that image, truly followed, will lead back to him. Holding the second—Neither is this Thou—"we see that every created thing, the highest devotion to moral duty, the purest conjugal love, the saint and the seraph, is no more than an image, that every one of them, followed for its own sake and isolated from its source, becomes an idol whose service is damnation."[133] These two ways, when reconciled, lead to an integrated faith that is neither gnostic nor materialistic.

Some word definitions might bring further clarity. Think of the words *eminence, imminence,* and *immanence.* As words on the page, they look significantly different. When spoken they sound almost indistinguishable, yet it is important to keep the differences in mind. Eminence speaks of one who has a large reputation. We can speak of a commencement speaker at a college graduation as the eminent Dr. So-and-So who has written many books and has loads of accomplishments and successes, but most of us know her because of a particular event in her life that has brought her to the forefront of our culture. We similarly address a king or queen as "Your Eminence." Another word is Imminence. It means "any minute" and if it helps to remember, has the abbreviation for minute (min.) right in the middle of the word. But Immanent speaks of that which is present. We remember it by seeing that the word *man* is in the middle of the word and recall, in the Incarnation, God the Son became a man and was present, dwelling within his creation. The word *immanence* is contrasted with the word *transcendent,* which is over and above, looming large and distant.

The statement "This also is Thou" speaks of divine immanence. It reminds us that God is present in the world he has made. We can speak of the *kataphatic.* The word *kata* is a Greek preposition

133 Lewis, *Arthurian Torso,* 151.

meaning down, or according to; it relates to the downward movement and manifestation of God toward creation and his presence in what he has made. We can speak of the divine immanence. There are Christian worship traditions that emphasize the affirmation of images. They participate in the romantic way. Everything seen in a world where God dwells is a call to worship. These traditions pray with eyes wide open. Worship is a sensuous experience. There are colors, smells, bells, even the taste of the bread and the wine. Some call it the Affirmative Way (or the *Via Affirmativa*). Images abound. The iconography pictures and embodies the reminder that we are not alone. God is with us. When this kind of worship is compromised, it moves toward idolatry. We begin to worship the very objects that evoked worship. In the legend of Arthur, Williams observes, "Lancelot is then the chief figure of the Way of Affirmations."[134] His fall occurs when he turns the thing that awakened his desire into the object of desire.

By contrast, the phrase "Neither is this Thou" speaks of the transcendence of God. God is more than the thing that evokes worship. Although he is present in the thing, he is more. He is bigger and beyond. Here we think of the *apophatic* approach to worship. *Apo* is the Greek preposition that means "from" or "away" and in this form of worship speaks of the upward and outward movement toward God. It prays with eyes closed. It shuts out all distractions to focus on the One. It is the Ascetic Way, also called the Way of Negation (or the *Via Negativa*). As the Way of Affirmation risks drifting toward idolatry, so the Way of Negation has its temptations; it tends to move toward rigidity and pharisaic practice. Imagine prayer before dinner in an apophatic household where one of the children says, "Mom, Johnny didn't have his eyes closed when we said grace before the dinner!" In that moment a little Pharisee is born. Williams and Lewis see the value of both ways.

134 Lewis, *Arthurian Torso*, 87.

When either way is compromised, the antidote is to enter into the practice of the other for a time. And the best way is to cultivate the reconciliation of the two ways in a unified, holistic approach.[135] Galahad and the Grail bring the apophatic and kataphatic forms together as one. The Grail reminds: open your eyes and behold. Yet, the Grail is not Christ, so close your eyes and think on him.

Bringing the Hidden to Light

The *Arthurian Torso* represents a labor of love by Lewis on behalf of his friend. It reveals how much the friendship mattered to him that he would put such effort into this work. It also reveals much source material that percolates into Lewis's own books. We have mentioned *The Great Divorce*, *Perelandra*, *That Hideous Strength*, *The Magician's Nephew*, and *The Lion, the Witch and the Wardrobe*. Various essays also come to mind including "The Weight of Glory," "The Inner Ring," and "Membership." The literary criticism Lewis wrote at the time also suggests some Williams influence. It would be fair to say that Lewis already had an interest in these ideas, and that friendship between the two men sharpened that interest to a point.

Regarding Lewis's critique of the poems as literature, he is not overly sanguine. He thinks the likelihood of eventual extinction of the poems is due to their obscurity. Nevertheless, Lewis does much to bring out of the depths that which was hidden from the light. If the poems do survive, he will be responsible for the resuscitation. His praises of the poems are that they contain "wisdom." They have about them a kind of "deliciousness" and "beauty." And they have strength of "incantation." Then Lewis asserts this high praise:

---

135 Note Jesus's remarks in Luke 7:33–35, "For John the Baptist has come eating no
     bread and drinking no wine; and you say, 'He has a demon!' The Son of Man has
     come eating and drinking; and you say, 'Behold a gluttonous man, and a drunkard,
     a friend of tax-gatherers and sinners!' Yet wisdom is vindicated by all her children."

If I say that in this respect it seems to me unequalled in modern imaginative literature, I am not merely recording the fact that I find many of Williams' doctrines appear to me to be true. I mean that he has re-stated to my imagination the very questions to which the doctrines are answers. Whatever truths or errors I come to hold hereafter, they will never be quite so abstract and jejune, so ignorant of relevant data, as they would have been before I read him.[136]

We can conclude by saying that no serious Charles Williams scholarship can afford to neglect this work where Lewis guides his readers in a most memorable exploration of Williams's big ideas. And no serious Lewis scholarship can neglect the impression left on Lewis by Williams.

136   Lewis, *Arthurian Torso*, 190–91.

Chapter 4

From Drab to Golden

English Literature in the Sixteenth Century excluding Drama

Lewis took many years to write *English Literature in the Sixteenth Century excluding Drama.* Similar to the Ancient Mariner in Coleridge's famous poem, Lewis found his book was like an albatross around his neck.

Eighteen years passed from the signing of the contract in 1935 until the volume was published by Oxford University Press. To finish the manuscript Lewis had to take a sabbatical. It was published in the series *The Oxford History of English Literature*, creating the opportunity for Lewis to later call it his OHEL volume.

The book is about 700 pages long, by far Lewis's most prolific work. Due to its length and its relative obscurity compared with his more popular publications, few (even among Lewis scholars) have actually read it. Therefore, it is easy to overlook its significance. But *English Literature in the Sixteenth Century excluding Drama* (or OHEL) gives students of Lewis an opportunity to peer firsthand into the plowing, weeding, and cultivating of the garden of his studies in medieval literature, and is important for all who would like an informed and seasoned guide to the literature of that age.

The Narrative Thread

To write this book, Lewis read every book written in English in the sixteenth century, and every book translated into English, in both the original language in which it was written (Latin, French, and Italian), and in translation, so his judgments might be properly informed and honestly made.[137] Dame Helen Gardner would watch him as he read and wrote in Duke Humfrey's Library at Oxford and observed, "It was an object lesson in what concentration meant. He seemed to create a wall of stillness around him."[138]

The challenge for Lewis—with such a wide array of books written across an entire century—was to make sense of the material and present it in a coherent and interesting way. Perhaps a biographer, when sorting through the teeming details of a life, faces a similar difficulty. When one imagines all of the thoughts and life experiences, relationships, learning and conversations, loves and interests, sorrows and struggles, and how these are processed by a single life, one can imagine the immense challenge. There is no such thing as a definitive biography. First, it could not be written. Second, it would be boring. The best biographies follow a narrative thread. There is a point the biographer wants to make, perhaps

---

137 Walter Hooper, *C. S. Lewis: A Companion and Guide* (New York: Harper Collins, 1996), 478.
138 Hooper, *C. S. Lewis*, 55.

even a lesson to be abstracted from all the detail honestly drawn. The author then limits the details selected to those that help tell the story that bears the suggested narrative. This does not mean the story is false, but that it is unpretentious. Lewis's narrative for OHEL is written along similar lines. There is no faulting the extent of his research, and he had to limit what he wrote to fulfill a narrative objective.

Lewis abstracts and divides the material into two major categories. In *Studies in Words* he said that literary judgments may be reduced to saying a work is either good or bad; after that, it is the burden of the critic to show in what way a thing is good or bad.[139] In OHEL, Lewis categorizes the books of the sixteenth century into two: the Drab and the Golden. In essence, the rest of the book is an explanation of why.

Definition of the Drab Age

"Drab, does not [necessarily] mean 'bad', but most Drab poetry had been bad in fact," writes Lewis.[140] He further describes drab poets by noting that the age "marks a period in which, for good or ill, poetry has little richness either of sound or images. The good work is neat and temperate, the bad flat and dry. There is more bad than good" among the drab authors.[141] When these authors are good, Lewis believes it is because they describe things well, at times even memorably. In these cases, the drab authors seek to imitate nature, to describe what is there. He gives examples that suggest his meaning, for example, observing about Scottish author William Dunbar's description of King James IV's mistress Margaret Drummond, "the absence of comment, or even apparent emotion, is the making of the poem. The setting, and the lady, seem to exist in their own right; we have simply been

---

139 Lewis, *Studies in Words* (New York: Cambridge University Press, 1960), 226–32.
140 Lewis, *English Literature in the Sixteenth Century: excluding Drama* (Oxford: Clarendon Press, 1954), 323.
141 Lewis, *English Literature in the Sixteenth Century*, 64.

shown something."[142] The author does not tell the reader what to feel, or think; he describes well and lets the reality begin to effect the accurate conclusions one ought to make if perceiving well. Similarly, Lewis writes about Norman Bradshaw that he "keeps his eye on the object,"[143] and it is in this regard that Lewis suggests the poem has a capacity to please the reader. Good descriptions of things as they are make for good philosophy, good moral and even emotional responses, and good literary criticism. Lewis has high praise for those who see things as they are, that is, as something apart from themselves.

As for the bad features of the Drab Age, Lewis writes, "The grand function of the Drab Age poets was to build a firm metrical highway out of the medieval swamp."[144] What did he mean by this? Here he criticizes one particular characteristic of the humanist movement coming alive in the sixteenth century that he believed distracted from the development of good literary art. Some explanation is necessary. The humanists, with the recovery of the Greek language and literature, began to prize the literary forms found in it. Consequently, they turned their backs on much that was medieval. In fact, Lewis says, the chief negative characteristic of the humanists "was a hatred of the Middle Ages."[145] Bound by conventions of style and holding in contempt their immediate progenitors, Lewis writes, "the schoolmen advanced, and supported, propositions about things: the humanists replied that his words were inelegant." He says it was characteristic of the humanists that "they jeer and do not refute."[146] This is not dissimilar to the kinds of dismissive *ad hominem* and *straw man* arguments heard so frequently in our own day and suggests another reason why Lewis's discussions still have substantive relevance.

142   Lewis, *English Literature in the Sixteenth Century*, 73.
143   Lewis, *English Literature in the Sixteenth Century*, 123.
144   Lewis, *English Literature in the Sixteenth Century*, 237.
145   Lewis, *English Literature in the Sixteenth Century*, 28.
146   Lewis, *English Literature in the Sixteenth Century*, 30.

Every age faces the temptation of untethering from the past as they engage in correcting the errors of their forebears. Every generation has plenty of faults, but reactions by one generation toward those who came before often become the material that inspires contempt from the emerging generation. Mere reaction inhibits the retention of any vestige of good that ought to be preserved even while filtering out the contemptible. Wisdom, on the other hand, cultivates the good seedling even as it pulls the weeds. The drab literature of the sixteenth century, as Lewis saw it, was dominated by the classical style and thereby truncated its own imaginative development.

Definition of the Golden Age

"The epithet *golden* is not eulogistic. By *golden* poetry I mean not simply good poetry, but poetry which is, so to speak, innocent or ingenuous," Lewis writes.[147] When he spoke of golden as innocent, he meant that it was unaffected by the cumbersome rigidity of the classical style. It was free to be more imaginative. To make his point, he explains that a general outlook on poetry lies behind the whole golden achievement. Some background is here necessary. "It is a defence not of poetry as against prose, but of fiction as against fact."[148] It is, as Lewis says, the right to make things up— or imagine that which is beyond the sensual—and perhaps in that imagining, seek to describe the transcendent or the immaterial.

In looking at the history out of which the Golden Age comes to maturity, Lewis recounts some of the history of Platonic-Aristotelian debates. While Plato expressed in the *Phaedrus* and in the *Ion* that inspiration may be behind poetry, this did not necessarily mean those inspired knew precisely what they were doing. They had simply been given a gift. Furthermore, in the *Republic*, Plato condemned representational art. He did not want

---

147 Lewis, *English Literature in the Sixteenth Century*, 64. Lewis repeats this distinction on 318.
148 Lewis, *English Literature in the Sixteenth Century*, 318.

Homer to be treated as encyclopedic or as a source for scientific certainty. Nature and the phenomenal world were a copy of the real and supersensuous world, Plato argued. Lewis writes, "Dialectic leads us up from unreal Nature to her original. But the arts which imitate Nature lead us down, further away from reality, to 'the copy of the copy.'" Lewis notes that there can be at least two responses to Plato. First the Aristotelian: "Poetry does not copy the particulars of Nature; it disengages and represents her general characteristics." Therefore, "It reveals the universal."[149]

Second, there was the Neo-Platonic answer. The image or icon is not the thing itself but grows out of "an image in the artist's mind." It is invented "Because wisdom and reason cannot be directly portrayed. Consequently, it shows forth the invisible by the visible."[150] Lewis writes of the work of Pheidias as an example. Pheidias was the Michelangelo of the classical age. He only sculpted the gods; his statues were those that decorated the temple on Mount Olympus, one of the Seven Wonders of the Ancient World. Lewis observes of Pheidias's statues, "Imagination made them, and she is a better artist than imitation; for where the one carves only what he has seen, the other carves what he has not seen." Lewis notes, "Pheidias used no visible model for his Zeus."[151]

A sensitivity to this kind of depiction is captured in Lewis's poem "Footnote to All Prayers." He sees something in prayer that is analogous to characteristics of the Golden Age as it reaches toward the imagined, known, but not seen:

He whom I bow to only knows to whom I bow
When I attempt the ineffable name, murmuring Thou;
And dream of Pheidian fancies and embrace in heart
Meanings, I know, that cannot be the thing thou art.
All prayers always, taken at their word, blaspheme,

149   Lewis, *English Literature in the Sixteenth Century*, 319.
150   Lewis, *English Literature in the Sixteenth Century*, 320.
151   Lewis, *English Literature in the Sixteenth Century*, 320.

Invoking with frail imageries a folk-lore dream;
And all men are idolaters, crying unheard
To senseless idols, if you take them at their word,
And all men in their praying, self-deceived, address
One that is not (so saith that old rebuke) unless
Thou, of mere grace, appropriate, and to thee divert
Men's arrows, all at hazard aimed, beyond desert.
Take not, oh Lord, our literal sense, but in thy great,
Unbroken speech our halting metaphor translate.[152]

Unencumbered by the rigidity of classical style, golden authors of the sixteenth century could capture more freely and imaginatively something of the transcendent, whether speaking theologically or writing about fairy or romance.

Lewis wrote in *The Allegory of Love* that the literary forms of personification and allegory were a means to describe the interior life—that is, to give it embodiment, and by means of story, provide the author the literary form necessary to write about the life of spiritual longing and romantic quest. We see this in Edmund Spenser's allegorizing of the virtues in *The Fairie Queene*, and it is in that regard that Lewis holds him up, along with Phillip Sidney, as two primary golden authors described in OHEL.

"Most of the golden poetry was not primarily intended either to reflect the actual world or to express the personality of the poet," Lewis says, adding, "The poets of that age were full of reverence—for God, for Kings, for fathers, for authority—but not of reverence for the actual." Furthermore, he captures the sentiment of the age: "For we are of higher birth than nature and her masters by divine right." Ethics were also portrayed and personified in the golden literature as something lovely and worthy of praise and adoration. Lewis remarks, "For virtue is lovely, not merely obligatory."[153]

152   Lewis, *The Pilgrim's Regress: An Allegorical Apology for Christianity, Reason, and Romanticism* (London: J. M. Dent and Sons, 1933), 183–84.
153   Lewis, *The Pilgrim's Regress*, 322.

New Learning and New Ignorance

Lewis's own literary aspiration was to write, in the golden manner, the very kind of literature that seeks to embody the transcendent as well as to capture the immaterial, unseen quest of the soul. Every age is a time of new learning and new ignorance. He begins OHEL with a description of the times, and these set the delimitations of his own study. He brings to mind the kinds of challenges that occurred in that century and reminds us of challenges that occur in the study of any era of history, for history is a fluid affair.

Cultures, the arts, politics, and social structures are always flowing like a river. To describe an era is like fixing a moment in a river's current. To describe it, to reduce the flow of history to a definitive moment, falsifies that very moment, for it neglects what came before and what followed after. Nevertheless, Lewis writes, "Though periods are a mischievous conception they are a methodological necessity."[154] What does he mean? Lewis literary scholar Bruce Edwards observed that the academic life consists of seeing patterns and exceptions. The patterns or generalizations make the passing on of a body of knowledge possible, but without accounting for the exceptions, the patterns are always false. Abstractions are helpful but never fully accurate.[155] Often this "mischievous conception," this "methodological necessity," as Lewis called it, had more to do with the observer than the observed. In Plato's *Theaetetus*, the mind is described analogically as being like a block of wax. Impressions made in the wax have to do with the quality of the wax. If the wax is too hard, no impression is made. If it is too soft, no lasting indent is retained. If the wax is full of impurities, the impression is distorted. The state of the perceiver is important to the process of receptivity. The perceiver must keep

154 Lewis, *The Pilgrim's Regress*, 64.
155 Professor Edwards made this observation to me in a conversation we had many years ago.

in mind that periods are not facts if he or she would benefit from abstractions. Nobody was running around in the Middle Ages saying, "I live in the Middle Ages." There is no crossing of a line from one period into another; there is nothing in the history of thought like a shoreline in geography.

The literature of the century was still medieval in form and spirit, but there were many new influences. Lewis counts several. There was a recovery of some knowledge of antiquity, particularly the recovery of Greek. With this came the interest in the "Classical Style" and the various rhetorical forms of expression. There came also a revived interest in the Greek manuscripts of the Bible, moving away from the dominance of the Latin Vulgate and a precise retuning of some theological traditions. The "New Theology" began to emerge, that is to say, the Reformation and religious controversy. More will be said about this later where Lewis gives special attention to discuss it.

Of the New Astronomy, that is, the major shift from the pre-Copernican world to the world defined by heliocentrism, Lewis observed that it had little effect on the literature of the age. He reminds his readers that the literary historian seeks to understand the time, not project onto the time what was emerging. We must not assume that what comes to be important in our day was of equal importance in the past. This may have been due to the fact that the late Middle Ages were far less materialistic than our present age seems to be. Supernaturalism still flourished. So the scientist, working with the merely measurable and quantifiable, would have had a far less elevated status in that age than in our own. Nevertheless, the literature of the sixteenth century seems unaffected by the emerging understanding of cosmology, and it is literature that is the focus of Lewis's study in OHEL. On the other hand, the New Geography excited slightly more interest than the new astronomy, and therefore its effects on the literature of that age is more apparent but not dramatic. However, Lewis reminds his readers that "the existence of America was one of the greatest disappointments in the history of Europe."[156] The Europeans were looking for trade routes to the east and North America was an impediment. What spoke most to the imagination was the myth of the "natural man" and the idea of the "Noble Savage."[157] The question, initially, led to projections more than conclusions and created prejudices among the later, so-called *enlightened* Europeans.

All the new discoveries occurring during the sixteenth century reveal that history is a pruning process. Some things, when proven false, must make way for the beliefs that will replace them. And some things once held dear, while not replaced by anything new, drift into oblivion simply because they are no longer valued. With new learning, as Lewis reminds us, there is always new ignorance. Sometimes there are gains and losses. What we must remember is that every age is destined to become a discarded image.

Highlights of OHEL

Let's now highlight key portions of OHEL that demonstrate facets of Lewis's narrative thread. He opens more than wardrobe doors, and OHEL is the threshold to many great works. One of the gifts Lewis gives to his readers is to awaken interest in a vast number of books with which they were never before acquainted. He lays a pathway to read the very works he describes. In this way, the neglected Lewis gives access to a liberal arts education.

THE CLOSE OF THE MIDDLE AGES IN SCOTLAND

What made the drab poets of Scotland so good was their ability to describe things as they were, and to describe them well. The material of the poet was the world around them. Therefore, to describe well was to write truly. And this could be used to entertain.

---

156   Lewis, *English Literature in the Sixteenth Century,* 1415.
157   Lewis, *English Literature in the Sixteenth Century,* 17.

Lewis appreciated the humor of many of these poets. He notes that much of the lyric poetry of Scotland might have been lost had it not been preserved for us in the anthologies so popularly produced. And he says that what these authors want from their audiences "is a hearty guffaw."[158] This required the authors to know their audience, and to tell their stories so they connected to the world where their readers and hearers lived each day. But the drab poets were not merely looking for a laugh. In one instance, as I've noted previously, Lewis writes of poet William Dunbar who wrote an elegant poem supposedly about King James IV's mistress, Margaret Drummond. He adds that "the absence of comment, or even of apparent emotion, is the making of the poem. The setting, and the lady, seem to exist in their own right; we have simply been shown something."[159] Lewis sees that this clarity of description connects with the reader and is in evidence in Gavin Douglas, David Lyndsay, and Alexander Scott. They are among the best of the drab age poets—by virtue of the fact that they can describe things as they are, and describe them well. The emotional response is not coerced; it follows naturally from the description. It renders to the image its due. The clear descriptions invited response, and generally, the response was one of enjoyment.

THE CLOSE OF THE MIDDLE AGES IN ENGLAND

While Lewis finds pleasure in the poetry of the close of the Middle Ages in Scotland, he is much less sanguine about the poetry in England at this time. His criticisms enable the reader of OHEL to mark the distinction more sharply between the good drab poetry and the bad. He writes, "We shall even find that the transition from poetical mastery to poetical imbecility as we come southward is a gradual one. . . . It is when we reach London that the really

---

158 Lewis, *English Literature in the Sixteenth Century,* 70.
159 Lewis, *English Literature in the Sixteenth Century,* 73.

bad work meets us."[160] Lewis comments, "In turning from the Scotch poetry of that age to the English we pass from civilization to barbarism."[161]

Here he sets forth standards for poetry. First, "Poetry must please." One flaw of late medieval English poetry is that it did not please. Of "The most perplexing and repellent feature of late medieval poetry in England, its metre," Lewis says, "the test lies in the ear." The patterns were too rigid and lacked fluidity. Lewis felt much of the drab poetry in England failed when it came to anything that might be considered delightful to the ear. Second, "no art lives by *nature*, only by acts of voluntary attention on the part of human individuals. When these are not made it ceases to exist."[162]

Careful attention should lead to an imitation of nature. Depictions can be imaginatively developed and expressed, but they do well to follow the suggestions of nature. Faithfulness to nature could inspire good drab poetry, but it still does not rise to what Lewis calls golden. In its response to nature, much of the late medieval English poetry simply failed. Consequently, the art form evident in the medieval allegory began to give way to something more rigid and forced in England.[163] For instance, of Thomas Sackville, Lewis notes, "He tears passions to tatters and endeavours to compensate for lack of real sympathy by mechanic exaggerations."[164] The material becomes cumbersome. The impress of an imagined literary style drawn from the classics and elevated by the humanists turned the late medieval authors away from their immediate medieval predecessors, and Lewis marks the loss. He goes so far as to say of Stephen Hawes that he was so completely affected by humanism that "his poetry has no intrinsic value."[165]

---

160   Lewis, *English Literature in the Sixteenth Century,* 121.
161   Lewis, *English Literature in the Sixteenth Century,* 120.
162   Lewis, *English Literature in the Sixteenth Century,* 123–24.
163   Lewis, *English Literature in the Sixteenth Century,* 237–45.
164   Lewis, *English Literature in the Sixteenth Century,* 244.
165   Lewis, *English Literature in the Sixteenth Century,* 129.

Furthermore, he writes, "It is another instance of that fatal flaw in humanism which draws a veil over Greek literature in the very act of discovering it." It did not accurately depict the Greek literature, and it rejected all that was pleasing of the medieval.[166] Lewis lays this decline at the feet of the influence of rigid form encouraged by the humanists. This became their standard of judgment and retarded the expression of potentially gifted artists. Lewis says, "This is the midwinter of our poetry; all smudge, blur, and scribble without a firm line or clear color anywhere."[167] In those rare cases where Lewis noted an expression of good drab poetry, it was when evidence of an imitation of nature was coupled with good description.

MICHAEL DRAYTON

Michael Drayton was one notable highlight at the close of the Drab Age. He becomes an example of Lewis directing attention to an author who will delight anyone willing to pick him up and read. Lewis's enthusiasm for Drayton lifts him from relative obscurity, and to discover Drayton through Lewis is to make a good introduction.

Drayton was born in Warwickshire in 1563. He secured a patronage and was sent to study at Oxford. Drayton published his first work in 1591 at age 28, and his last book at 57 in 1630. He died in 1631, and his remains were buried at Westminster Abby. Most readers of Lewis generally will not have heard of Drayton unless they have a formal education in English literature. However, one who reads OHEL cannot help but notice Lewis's praise for Drayton. Lewis writes, "His imagery of Voyage, Phoenix, Star, and River (he was enamoured of rivers all of his life) mediate something not inconsistent with human passion, but going beyond it."[168] He

---

166   Lewis, *English Literature in the Sixteenth Century,* 132.
167   Lewis, *English Literature in the Sixteenth Century,* 127.
168   Lewis, *English Literature in the Sixteenth Century,* 496.

shared an affinity with Drayton at this point, for Lewis himself was deeply attracted to ideas that highlighted the matter of the soul longing for its proper home, its ultimate lover, and longing to have the broken things within repaired and restored.

As a case in point, Lewis quotes from Drayton's Sonnet VI, "How Many Paltry, Foolish, Painted Things":

> How many paltry, foolish, painted things,
> That now in coaches trouble every street,
> Shall be forgotten, whom no Poet sings,
> Ere they be well wrapt in their winding-sheet!
> Where I to thee eternity shall give,
> When nothing else remaineth of these days,
> And *Queens hereafter shall be glad to live*
> *Upon the alms of thy superfluous praise.*
> Virgins and matrons, reading these my rhymes,
> Shall be so much delighted with thy story
> That they shall grieve they lived not in these times,
> To have seen thee, their sex's only glory.
> > So shalt thou fly above the vulgar throng,
> > Still to survive in my immortal song.[169]

Lewis writes of the italicized lines above that if Drayton "had never written another verse, these two lines would secure him that praise which is due to men who have done some one thing to perfection."[170] In Lewis's judgment, those two lines were enough to put Drayton into the class of Golden. It is also a fine example of the kinds of treasures one might find in these neglected works of Lewis.

169 Michael Drayton, *Poems of Michael Drayton*, "Idea 1619" (London: George Newnes, Limited, 1905), 207–08. Italics mine.

170 Lewis, *English Literature in the Sixteenth Century*, 497.

Lewis observes that the Protestant Reformation occurred across three planes: "firstly in the thought and conscience of the individual, secondly in the intertangled realms of ecclesiastical and political activity, and thirdly on the printed page."[171] Each plane stands in relation to the others, but for the purposes of his book, Lewis focuses primarily on the published page. People of conviction stood on both sides of the religious divide throughout the contentious sixteenth century, and most were affected by the influences of classicism. Therefore, the writers on religious themes were, in Lewis's estimate, drab. Some were good drab, and many were bad.

Many of the Catholics and Reformers whom Lewis assesses, for the sake of conscience, suffered martyrdom. Their courage of conviction is not up for scrutiny, but rather, their capacity to write. Lewis also notes that conscience is not always a good clarifier of truth for "those who were burned as heretics were often (and, on their premises, logically) eager to burn others on the same charge."[172] Among the Catholics discussed are John Colet (1467?–1519), John Fisher (1459–1535), and Thomas More (1478–1535). Lewis classifies Colet's written work as middling between bad drab and good. He was a reasonable man aware of the abuses in the ecclesiastical community but sought to expose them rather than divide the Church. As far as any significant literary achievement, "He helped to banish the old allegorical method of interpretation."[173] As a humanist he is graded as drab, but Lewis says his real weakness was less as a Churchman than as a Platonist.[174] Lewis reminds, "A cloistered perfectionist, who happens to be also a rhetorician often says, not exactly more than he means, but more than he understands."[175]

171   Lewis, *English Literature in the Sixteenth Century,* 157.
172   Lewis, *English Literature in the Sixteenth Century,* 39.
173   Lewis, *English Literature in the Sixteenth Century,* 159.
174   Lewis, *English Literature in the Sixteenth Century,* 162
175   Lewis, *English Literature in the Sixteenth Century,* 159.

Fisher was the Bishop of Rochester, and he was martyred. Lewis says his work falls under the classification good drab by virtue of his true character. He says of his published work that his style "is grave and a little diffuse, never comic."[176] There is a medieval sweetness and richness that hangs about his prose, and Lewis claims that "he is hardly ever at all scurrilous. . . . And compared with More, or even Tyndale, Fisher is almost courteous."[177] However, "His chief weakness is that he is too leisurely: he is in no hurry to end a sentence or to let an idea go."[178] This was characteristic of the drab, humanist tendency.

More, also a martyr and a man of conscience, Lewis says, was bad drab largely due to his humanist rigidity of style coupled with his legal mind. He adds that it is proper to consider him a major British author on the merits of his *Utopia*. Nevertheless, "Of his English prose, as a whole, great claims are not in order. It is neither concise nor full; it has neither lightning thrusts nor a swelling tide of thought and feeling. As for his sanctity, to live and die like a saint is no doubt a better thing than to write like one, but it is not the same thing; and More does not write like a saint." In religious argument, "To rebuke magnificently is one of the duties of a great polemical writer. More often attempts it but he always fails. He loses himself in a wilderness of opprobrious adjectives. He cannot denounce like a prophet; he can only scold and grumble like a father in an old fashioned comedy."[179] Lewis adds, "He multiplies words in a vain endeavor to stop up all possible chinks. . . . The style is stodgy and dough-like."[180]

Five Protestant Reformers provide enough of a sample to show that their convictions as men did not make them great writers. The influence of the humanist's classical style is the very weakness of

176 Lewis, *English Literature in the Sixteenth Century*, 161.
177 Lewis, *English Literature in the Sixteenth Century*, 164.
178 Lewis, *English Literature in the Sixteenth Century*, 162.
179 Lewis, *English Literature in the Sixteenth Century*, 175–76.
180 Lewis, *English Literature in the Sixteenth Century*, 180.

their literary form. For example, Lewis considers William Tyndale (?–1536), Hugh Latimer (1485–1555), Thomas Cranmer (1489–1556), and John Knox (1505–1572) each in turn. Three of the four were martyred. Tyndale, Lewis says, is good drab. He is inferior to More in use of humor, but superior in overall style. He is not as many-sided as More but tends to be joyful and lyric in his poetic quality. Lewis acknowledges the influence of Tyndale's translation of the Bible and how it was used in many of its expressions in the translations that followed in its wake. This, for Lewis, marked Tyndale's real achievement. Lewis says he is not particularly interested in commenting so much on the merits of the theology of these religious writers, but he does say of Tyndale: "The idea that his doctrine of faith dispensed a man from works is a gross misunderstanding. They are not, for him, the cause of salvation, but they are its inseparable symptom. We are 'loosed from the law'—by fulfilling it. 'Deedes are the fruites of love and love is the fruit of fayth.'"[181] Here is one of the places where Lewis shows his colors and highlights a theological point of view.

Latimer was also good drab. Lewis has great respect and appreciation for Latimer, especially his sermons, and says of his congregation, "He establishes intimacy with them in order to sway them. It is a well understood homiletic technique which descends to him from the Middle Ages (his method has affinities with that of Chaucer's Pardoner) and which has survived into our own days." Lewis then gives an example: "'Young feller', said General Booth [founder of the Salvation Army] to Kipling, 'if I thought I could win one more soul to the Lord by playing the tambourine with my toes, I'd—I'd learn how.' The only test which Latimer would admit as relevant for his sermons was their practical efficacy. And they were efficacious." His sermons may not be good literature, Lewis remarks, but by virtue of the responses he received, they contained a literary virtue.[182]

---

181 Lewis, *English Literature in the Sixteenth Century*, 189.
182 Lewis, *English Literature in the Sixteenth Century*, 193–94.

Thomas Cranmer is classified as good drab primarily for his work on the Prayer Book, but other than this significant contribution, Lewis was unimpressed. But he adds, "The Prayer Book is the one glory of the Drab Age."[183]

Of all of the Reformers, however, Lewis is least complimentary to John Knox. He says he is bad drab, by virtue not only of his manner, but his matter. Whenever Knox says something that has merit, Lewis says others most often said it better. He has little room for Knox, calling him "a self-ignorant man" and "most embarrassing."[184] And after discussing Knox, Lewis says, "Behind every system of sixteenth-century thought, however learnedly it is argued, lurks cruelty."[185]

The Matter of Translation

As to the work of translation (both scholarly and literary), Lewis makes several observations. He says, "The business of the translator is to write down what he thinks the original meant."[186] Lewis honestly observes that people like Thomas More and William Tyndale came to the word *ekklesia* (or church) with a preconception of what the church was, or should be, and that this affected the way they did translation concerning the doctrine of the church. Tyndale did not want to translate the word "church" because he did not believe that what passed for church in his day was what Paul had in mind when he wrote. On the other hand, More believed that the church as it was in his day was exactly what Paul had in mind. Thus, the views of the translators could, and certainly here did, affect translation. Lewis concludes, "Translation, by its very nature, is a continuous implicit commentary."[187] He points out that of those doing translation work in the sixteenth century, "All

183   Lewis, *English Literature in the Sixteenth Century*, 194–95, 204.
184   Lewis, *English Literature in the Sixteenth Century*, 198–99.
185   Lewis, *English Literature in the Sixteenth Century*, 200–01.
186   Lewis, *English Literature in the Sixteenth Century*, 206.
187   Lewis, *English Literature in the Sixteenth Century*, 206.

parties were agreed that the Bible was the oracles of God."[188] The care taken by those translators who have reverence for Scripture will generally be in evidence. Nevertheless, doctrinal proclivities held before translating a passage are likely to affect the work. If a translator begins to apply his high doctrine of Scripture to his translation, making it equal with the actual word of God, troubles could follow. How easy it is to dismiss the thought of another once we are tempted to equate our word or even our translations as equal to the word of God. This can happen in theological debates, whether during the religious controversies of the sixteenth century, or in our own time. The wise will learn from the past.

There were also positive examples, often overlooked, from the period of Lewis's review. There were Protestant and Catholic translators, and there were ancient texts in need of translation. Judgments could be made as to the fairness of the translations. The appeal was to the available texts themselves; faithfulness to these texts could be checked and rechecked. Lewis believes that if a comparison needs to be made "on almost any view, Tyndale who inaugurated, and the Genevan translators who first seriously advanced, our tradition, tower head and shoulders above all others." Of the Roman Catholics, Lewis offers praise for Gregory Martin, working at "the English College of Douay (temporarily housed at Rheims from where this translation derives its name)."[189] Martin was:

. . . a lecturer in Hebrew, and sometime scholar of St. John's Oxford. The Council of Trent in 1546 had pronounced the Vulgate to be the only authentic Latin version and Martin worked from it, not from the original. This, however, does not by any means remove his work from serious consideration; he had the Greek also before him, he used the Geneva, and was himself used by the Authorized Version.[190]

188 Lewis, *English Literature in the Sixteenth Century*, 212.
189 Lewis, *English Literature in the Sixteenth Century*, 211.
190 Lewis, *English Literature in the Sixteenth Century*, 211–12.

This cross-pollination between Catholic and Protestant translators is an interesting fact, often neglected, but noted by Lewis as significant. Whatever the theological differences, those doing serious academic work in translation still had respect for the clear scholarly diligence of the other. Both the scholars of the Catholic and the Protestant traditions used material produced by the others. This benefited the translators even where the sides represented were in antipathy. "Even a few hours spent in actual collation will, I think, leave the impression that the vast majority of variants result neither from differences in doctrine nor from literary taste but from the steady advance of scholarship."[191] Even the Authorized Version (KJV 1611), Lewis believes, has not had its debts to both Geneva and Rheims sufficiently acknowledged.[192]

Lewis is one of the very few who read thoroughly both sides of the Reformation literature. Consequently, his judgments in these matters are more nuanced and reserved. He concludes his observations with these words: "Each Party increasingly misunderstood the other and triumphed in refuting positions which their opponents did not hold: Protestants misrepresenting Romans as Pelagians or Romans misrepresenting Protestants as Antinomians."[193]

The Golden Age

Here, finally, we have Philip Sidney and Edmund Spenser. Lewis held up these two as the best examples of golden. The reason is not merely their gifts of description, but their ability to give imaginative embodiment to the interior life. They sought to awaken aspirations that looked beyond the mere empirical, sensory world, thus giving voice to transcendent desire. Their work, awakening desire, gives their readers the hope that joy and fulfillment might one day become a reality.

Spenser particularly, through *The Fairie Queene*, awakens longing for a life of virtue. He is first a storyteller. His manner is

191 Lewis, *English Literature in the Sixteenth Century*, 212–13.
192 Lewis, *English Literature in the Sixteenth Century*, 213–14.
193 Lewis, *English Literature in the Sixteenth Century*, 37.

unaffected by the humanist rigidity. His story, on the surface, is not the whole story. Lewis says, "His tranquility is a robust tranquility that 'tolerates the indignities of time', refusing to be deceived by them, recognizing them as truths, indeed, but only the truths of 'a foolish world'. He would not have called himself the poet of our waking dreams': rather the poet of our waking." His stories create in his readers the desire to re-enter his made-up world again and again. Each visit to the world he imagines for his readers nudges them to see in themselves the hope of something better. Lewis says, "I never met a man who says that he *used* to like the *Faerie Queene.*"[194]

A Golden Thread

Lewis read and commented on virtually every English writer of the age. This massive book of his could easily have turned into something like reading a laundry list. Yet it holds one's attention. Why is this so?

A smart sense of humor runs through the book, page after page. More importantly, the thread of those very qualities Lewis defines as Golden are woven throughout his own manuscript. He models the best of what he loved about the period. If the book ever bogs down it is only in some of the drab sections, where Lewis's manner matches his matter. But in his own writing in OHEL, the golden style is frequently in evidence. He describes things well and is always clear. He is a master of depiction and metaphors to make his points, and his good humor appears on nearly every page. Furthermore, he seeks, as he does in all his books, to awaken desire in the hearts of his readers for other worlds. In OHEL, that other world was the English sixteenth century, but he applies similar gifts as a writer and creator when he turns to his science fiction trilogy and to *Narnia.* Those who really want to know Lewis and his world must read *English Literature in the Sixteenth Century.*

194   Lewis, *English Literature in the Sixteenth Century,* 393.

The common room in Lewis's home, the Kilns, where he did much of his reading and entertained many literary friends, including J. R. R. Tolkien.

Photo courtesy of Mark Neal.

Chapter 5

Unlocking the Doors of Language

Studies in Words

Studies in Words is a word-hoard of word histories. A dense, scholarly work, it is not for the faint of heart. Published in 1960, it was originally a series of lectures delivered to students at Cambridge University. Lewis's purpose in writing was to facilitate a more accurate reading of old books. It examines the histories of ten words and how their meaning has changed over time. These ten words are nature, sad, wit, free, sense, simple, conscience and conscious, world, life, and "I dare say." Lewis notes that an increased accuracy in reading illumines the ideas and sentiments of different times in which a word was used.

But why study these word histories at all? For Lewis, old books give us a standard by which to judge more modern works. They help to correct the characteristic mistakes and blindness of our own period. If we read new books only, he asseverates, we increase the blindness and weaken our guard against it. "The only palliative is to keep the clean sea breeze of the centuries blowing through our minds, and this can be done only by reading old books," he writes.[195] This kind of word study is vital to understanding what an author of a certain period meant.[196]

He writes that we cannot separate philology—the structural and historical understanding of language—from a study of literature. Those who desire to do this "are either crying for the moon or resolving on a lifetime of persistent and carefully guarded delusion."[197] Again, understanding a word's meaning-history helps us to read accurately the work of a particular era. If we only bring our own understanding of a word or words to a poem, it is likely that we will misread and so misunderstand what the author meant. We get our poem, not the poem the poet intended. Thus, the wise reader examines the semantic histories of words.

But who among us has the time or inclination for this kind of exacting study? Perhaps there are some. We can certainly read old works and enjoy them, but if Lewis is right, then we will have to be content to misread, because most of us won't take the time to do the research that will lead to a more accurate reading of a text. But that is why we need guides. Our own intelligence and sensibility are not enough. Lewis himself acts as a guide, and not just to word histories. Many of his works reflect this cartographical impulse: *The Discarded Image, Studies in Medieval and Renaissance Literature, Spenser's Images of Life, The Allegory of Love.* Each helps facilitate a greater understanding of a given period so we might read its literature and appreciate its art more accurately.

195 Lewis, *God in the Dock*, "On the Reading of Old Books" (Grand Rapids, MI: Eerdmans, 1970), 202.
196 Lewis, *Studies in Words*, 3.
197 Lewis, *Studies in Words*, 3.

Lewis ultimately desires a responsibility toward language, an idea that is largely unfamiliar in our modern age. Language equals communication, therefore the more nuance in its words, the better the communication. This responsibility entails an awareness of what we are doing when we use language ourselves and when we engage with language of the past.

The reader may ask how a work like *Studies in Words* can have any impact given our current cultural inclinations. Who will actually engage texts in this way? It is a seemingly lost skill. In a culture that denigrates this kind of responsibility, and where language care has become vestigial, how can this book still be relevant? How can we learn from it? We may give lip service to caring about language, but we remain caught up in technological advances that render its nuance and importance more and more obsolete, seemingly irrelevant, even laughable. Keep these questions in the back of your mind, and we'll return to them later.

As Lewis gives a rationale for how we can think about language ethically, we must also examine how language decays and dies, and to what extent we participate in this death.

Because of the exacting and highly detailed nature of this work, we will primarily examine Lewis's understanding of the principles of language change over time and let the reader explore the word histories when they have leisure to read the book.

Principles of Meaning Change in Language

As we think about responsibility to language, it is essential, then, to understand how meaning changes in language over time. It is in this way that we may begin our study of word histories and so improve our chances of reading old books more accurately. Lewis outlines seven principles of meaning change that give us a sort of ethical framework for how we can think about and use language more responsibly. It is a series of ways to cultivate attentiveness to what we are doing when we speak and write. We will briefly outline them here.

The first principle is what Lewis calls *ramification*. This happens when words take on new meanings over time. He likens it to a tree throwing out new branches. At times new branches will overshadow and kill old ones, but not always. We may often find the earliest senses of a word continuing to be used for centuries despite the intervening years of new growth of senses that might have been expected to obliterate them. Thus, the word becomes a sort of palimpsest. Lewis further adds that most people don't know about the tree and don't care about it. Perhaps he sensed the dwindling responsibility he was advocating toward language that would relegate it to the purview of philologists and other such specialists. When we are using one word in many different senses, we are participating in the effects of this semantic ramification, though we mostly aren't even aware of it, because to begin with, we are not aware of the tree.[198]

A second principle of meaning change is the *insulating power of the context*. This enables a speaker to give many meanings to one word without the danger of confusion. And the reason we don't get confused, Lewis notes, is that we don't often encounter these words in the same context. For example, when we see a sign for "Wine and Spirits" we are not thinking of ghosts or devils or angels because the context provides the appropriate sense of the word to our minds.[199]

The third principle, he writes, is the *dangerous sense*. Every word has a dominant sense that lies uppermost in our minds. The danger is that whenever we come across this word we are more than likely to give it this sense. This is particularly risky when we are reading an old work and we automatically read this sense into a word when an old author meant something different. Thus, we misread.[200]

The fourth principle centers around the *distinction between what a word means and what a speaker (or writer) means by a*

---

198 Lewis, *Studies in Words*, 9–10.
199 Lewis, *Studies in Words*, 11.
200 Lewis, *Studies in Words*, 13.

word. Lewis gives a good example. Consider two friends going to the theater. One of them mentions that they should have supper after the performance. One friend meant by "supper" a biscuit and a mug of cocoa, while the other was thinking of a cold bird and a bottle of wine. The problem is that if the speaker's meaning becomes common, it can, over time, become the word's meaning. This is one of the effects of semantic ramification.[201]

Fifth are what Lewis terms *tactical definitions.* This occurs when a group or party attempts to define a potent word for one side and to deny it to the other. These definitions usually do not conform to actual usage and are used purely to exclude something that is disliked or to take down some enemy. It is a practice of exclusion, even of inner ring mentality. Tactical definitions don't give information about the actual meaning of a word; they are appropriated and a different meaning is forced on them. We will return to discuss this particular principle in more depth.[202]

Sixth is the *methodological idiom.* It describes how one word that refers to different things can produce ambiguity. An example would be the word "history." It can often be difficult, Lewis writes, to know if the word means past events themselves or the study that attempts to understand them. Failure to recognize this principle in action can result in muddled interpretations.

The final principle revolves around *moralization of status-words.* This occurs when a word that referred to a person's rank tends to become a word that assigns a certain character and behavior to that person. Those that describe a superior rank can become terms of praise. Those that describe an inferior rank can become terms of disapproval. An example is found in the word "gentleman." This word used to refer to a member of a certain social class. Gradually it came to have an ethical sense and be associated only with one's behavior, how one acted in certain instances.[203]

201 Lewis, *Studies in Words*, 14–15.
202 Lewis, *Studies in Words*, 19.
203 Lewis, *Studies in Words*, 20–21.

If we are aware—insofar as we are capable of doing so—of these seven principles when we speak and write, we will participate in that responsibility toward words and language and ultimately meaning that Lewis advocates. The result could be a clarity of thought and a nuanced understanding that creates depth and stability in discourse and writing, rather than the destabilization that these days is affecting language at every level of communication. But in the meantime, without our knowledge, we are also contributing to the death of language every day, so it is as well to look more closely at how this can happen.

The Death of Language

All of us have contributed at some level to verbicide, the death of language. This death is not the eradication of a word; it occurs when a word takes on a plethora of meanings and so becomes meaningless for purposes of communication. Lewis describes four ways verbicide can occur. First of all, through inflation. For example, substituting "awfully" for "very," or "awesome" to express approval for anything. Second, through verbiage, the use of a word as an inherent promise that won't be kept. Lewis gives the example of someone using the word "significant" and then never telling us what a thing is significant of. A third way we can contribute to verbicide is through using words as party banners, appropriating the selling quality of the word. Examples would include substituting "whig" and "tory" for "liberal" and "conservative." Finally, the greatest cause of verbicide, according to Lewis, is that our words can become less descriptive and more evaluative. He suggests we are often more eager to express approval or disapproval rather than describe something. For example, think of the number of synonyms we use to express simply good or bad. A partial list would include terrible, awful, horrible, great, awesome, terrific. If we were to examine the histories of these words, we would find that each had a specific meaning to be used as a specific descriptor in a given context.

Now all these words have become evaluative, and therefore they have lost their meaning and really mean nothing.[204] Lewis admonishes us to be aware of these things and resolve never to commit verbicide. But this injunction is increasingly difficult to follow. As our language erodes due to cultural shifts in media and societal devaluation, who would even understand the correct context in which to use the word *awesome?* It rolls off the tongue as a descriptor for just about anything. And we all do it because it is culturally acceptable. Perhaps it would be better to refrain from speech than to use one of these catch-all words. There is an ethics involved in how we speak and use language and we believe Lewis is calling us to this ethical approach.

Verbicide ultimately leads to a loss of communication as well as to the dehumanization of those on the receiving end. Lewis writes that one of the most important and effective uses of language is the emotional use. We don't communicate only to reason or inform, but to love, quarrel, rebuke, console, and so forth. And this emotion is best aroused through addressing the imagination, as the poets do so well. And there is a distinction between language that arouses versus language that expresses emotion. Language that arouses produces an effect on the hearer; language that expresses discharges our emotion.[205]

But, Lewis says, categories exist which are purely emotional. The vocabulary of endearment, complaint, and abuse are examples. In these vocabularies, there is no appeal to the imagination, so there is no function but to express or stimulate emotion. For example, the word "damn" began with the whole of the Christian eschatology behind it and ended as a word empty of content, as merely an imprecation. But it began with imaginative content. A word like *damn* becomes weaker when it loses its content and its imaginative connection to this eschatology, so it ceases to have power even

204   Lewis, *Studies in Words,* 7.
205   Lewis, *Studies in Words,* 314–19.

as an imprecation.[206] Again, to be effective, language must not be solely emotional; it must connect to the imagination. Once it becomes solely emotional, it ceases to be language and performs no function. In the case of the word *damn* it serves no function but to tell us that the speaker has lost his temper.[207]

Up to this point, Lewis doesn't see this devolution of language as a problem. The real problem, the real corruption, he notes, comes when the purpose in speaking is purely emotional, but this fact is concealed from others by words that seem to be, but are not, charged with emotional content. Examples of this would be bolshevist, fascist, Jew, capitalist, bourgeois, racist, and so forth. These are used merely as words of contempt.[208] They have been given tactical definitions.

As Lewis outlines how language dies, hopefully we have a clearer sense of how words lose power as language to communicate meaning but can gain power for purposes of propaganda and control when anyone can snatch a term and foist their own meaning upon it.

Tactical Definitions

We glanced quickly at the seven principles of meaning change outlined by Lewis, but we want to isolate and expand on tactical definitions. We believe this term is more readily relatable and also concerns our present culture more closely. Lewis himself expounded on this principle in several of his works, so it would appear that he valued its importance as well.

We described earlier two causes of verbicide, or the murder of a word. One was inflation or deification; the other, appropriating a word for its selling quality. Both of these would be part of what constitutes a tactical definition. But how does a word come to be in a deified or inflated position and how does it then become tactical?

---

206 Lewis, *Studies in Words*, 320–22.
207 Lewis, *Studies in Words*, 323.
208 Lewis, *Studies in Words*, 325.

Let's look at an example. One of the words Lewis examines in *Studies in Words* is "life." He outlines many of the word's different senses, but we will focus on life in the biological sense. This may be defined as what is common to all organisms: organization, nutrition, growth and reproduction.[209] We will hereafter refer to this as *Life (Biological)*.

Lewis then describes for us the picture of evolution. He calls it a great myth: *Life (Biological)* begins as nothing with all the odds against it, then gradually it becomes man. Though he didn't believe in naturalistic evolution, Lewis found the picture moving. He writes that "it invites us first to reify, then to personify, finally to deify *Life (Biological)*."[210] This three-step process ends in an abstraction that is valued almost in the same way as a physical manifestation of reality. He writes that we engage in this deification because we fear death—our own and that of our loved ones. We want life to endure forever, to be the hero of the story. The problem is that this deification can have dangerous ramifications down the line. It can be used to rationalize evil acts in the name of preserving life. Lewis writes about this very idea in *That Hideous Strength*.

The American scholar Richard Weaver notes in his book *The Ethics of Rhetoric* that societies embrace high concepts or ideals. In rhetoric, these are called ultimate or "god" terms. "Justice" or "love" might be ultimate ideals. In the past, words like "progress" or "American" have functioned as god terms.[211] Today, "technology" is one of our primary god terms. The problem with god terms is that they can become tactical terms; they are inflated beyond what they deserve and we think of them as the highest good. The danger is that this may lead to groupthink, which sacrifices independent thinking and gives its members an illusion of invulnerability.

---

209 Lewis, *Studies in Words*, 294.
210 Lewis, *Studies in Words*, 303.
211 Richard Weaver, *The Ethics of Rhetoric* (Chicago: Henry Regnery Company, 1953), 213–18.

For example, consider screen technologies. We talk about them, we work on them, live on them, integrate them into every facet of our lives. There is a kind of blind acceptance that whatever newest technology we are given must be good and necessary. Yet there are very few dissenting voices. We go with the flow. "Technology," once it is accepted in this way, can be used to rationalize all sorts of morally and ethically questionable activities and advances.

Rhetoric, rightly used, attempts to move others toward the highest ideal, Weaver states.[212] But it can be used for ill purposes as well. Plato's sophists were expert rhetoricians; their language was artistically contrived but possessed very little meaning. German philosopher Josef Pieper writes that one of the things language accomplishes is to convey reality.[213] He notes that any time language disregards reality, communication ceases and the receivers are dehumanized.[214] French philosopher Jacques Ellul believed that language is what essentially humanizes us. When we don't have an ethical approach to how we use language, we end up abusing it and others.

This leads us back to Weaver, who states that another type of ultimate term, the charismatic term, is one that has become irrational and had its authority forced upon it. For example, in World War II, the term "war effort" was used to rationalize much that people would not normally put up with. "Infidel" would have been such a term in the Middle Ages.[215] The idea of "master race" would have been another for Nazi Germany. The function of a charismatic term is to manipulate people and create groupthink and propaganda.

We've mentioned that words that have been appropriated as tactical or have become charismatic terms can have dangerous

---

212   Weaver, *The Ethics of Rhetoric*, 25.
213   Josef Pieper, *Abuse of Language, Abuse of Power* (San Francisco: Ignatius Press, 1992), 15.
214   Pieper, *Abuse of Language, Abuse of Power*, 21.
215   Weaver, *The Ethics of Rhetoric*, 227–31.

ramifications. Lewis is likely thinking about this when he writes about the appropriation of the idea of *Life (Biological)* in *That Hideous Strength.* Think back to *Out of the Silent Planet.* Why do Weston and Devine travel to Malacandra? Their goal is to find a place to which the human race can relocate once it has destroyed the earth. Here is the idea of the preservation of life at all costs. In *That Hideous Strength*, we see the fruition of this continuance of life in the idea of *sanitation,* a seemingly innocuous word that has been seized as a party banner and given a tactical definition. That is, a definition not original to the word has been forced upon it. It has become a charismatic term as outlined by Weaver; all of life can be defined in relation to it. Thus, police forces are called "sanitary executives." And eventually the nefarious plan of the N.I.C.E. is revealed through the ultimate use of the term *sanitation*: to eradicate all organic life. Humans are to evolve simply as mind. Here we see how such terms can come to have such devastating power and control to the point of altering whole societies.

Unlocking the Doors

So why should we care about any of this? What about this book is important for the modern Lewis reader? First of all, this work, even though it is one of Lewis's more abstruse books, gives us a new appreciation for the ways he valued and was committed to using language rightly. He insists that the reason we should care to do so is that knowing accurate definitions enables us to enter into a work with understanding of what an author meant when the work was written. Modern reader-response criticism would have no place here, because what we bring to the text is not the kind of reading that Lewis is advocating. He hopes that we can shed our own personalities, worldviews, and preconceptions and try, as much as we are able, to enter into the period of whatever literature we are reading and see it through the eyes of the characters in the story. This enables us to enter the author's world, to be more fully immersed and to see how the world looked through that author's eyes. Lewis was a proponent of the broader view that enables us to see the world through another's eyes, and this exercise hopefully helps us see our own age with greater clarity.

Second, if we focus again on this theme of understanding tactical definitions and how they relate to meaning change, we can perhaps answer the questions that we posited at the beginning of this chapter: how can this book be relevant for us now? Jacques Ellul believed that language was at the root of what it meant to be human. Writing in the 1960s, Ellul blamed the prevalence of the image for what he called the "humiliation of the word," the emptying from language of meaning or nuance. James van der Laan, a professor at Illinois State University, calls this emptying "plastic language." This is language that has been divested of moral overtones and made to apply to any situation.[216] Lewis writes about this very idea in his essay "Bluspels and Flalansferes." This is a similar idea to Weaver's charismatic terms. Plastic language eliminates complexity and makes language more efficient. Yet Lewis believed language should be nuanced and complex. Efficiency results in a loss of nuance and meaning, and thus we are more prone to fall victim to propaganda and schemes of control without being aware of it.

Ellul defines propaganda as the synthesizing of contentment and distraction. Our digital technologies perform this function admirably well. We are enmeshed deeply in levels of propaganda we can't even begin to understand: invisible and silent methodologies, menu-driven interfaces, advertising and marketing tactics and more that are all designed to synthesize contentment and distraction. Consider your Amazon account. Amazon's algorithm works to understand your purchasing habits and then customizes messaging or other products that you might be interested in. How many of us have ended up purchasing things we weren't intending to buy because

---

216   J. M. van der Laan, "Plastic Words: Words Without Meaning," *Bulletin of Science, Technology & Society*, 21, no. 5 (2001): 350–351.

of Amazon's suggestions? We don't see this as propaganda, but as ease and accessibility. Yet anytime algorithms are working to predict and finally dictate our behavior, we have succumbed to propaganda. We have followed someone else's menu or been manipulated without awareness. And awareness is precisely what Lewis is advocating for as we seek to understand the meanings of words.

It all begins with language, with using the selling quality of words like *technology* to be the cure-all for every ill. Evgeny Morozov calls this technological solutionism, or "the will to improve just about everything," even to the creation of solutions where there are no problems.[217] And this is why this book is so important. It makes us aware of the potency of words and how they can be used and manipulated with massive ramifications. Becoming aware of these issues as they relate to language alone makes reading this book worthwhile.

Let me provide an example that will hopefully cement what we've been outlining here. Most of us will likely have an instant and visceral response to the following symbol:

We all know this to be the symbol of Hitler's Nazi regime. But browse a shelf of old books and you might discover a volume of Rudyard Kipling. Kipling was an English author who spent the first five years of his life in India before he was shipped off to an English boarding school. He is perhaps most well-known for writing *The Jungle Book*. Certain editions of Kipling are embossed with this sort of seal on the cover:

217 Evgeny Morozov, *To Save Everything, Click Here* (New York: Public Affairs, 2013), 5.

It contains an image of an elephant holding a lotus flower in its trunk and a swastika in the upper left quadrant of the image. If you compare this with the Nazi symbol, you'll notice they aren't exactly alike; the prongs face in different directions. Nevertheless, they are both swastikas and unless you were a close observer, you wouldn't likely notice the difference. In Kipling's time, a decade or more before the Nazi rise in Germany, the swastika was an ancient eastern religious symbol that had been around for thousands of years. For Kipling, this was nothing more than a good luck symbol. In later editions of his books, Kipling made sure it was removed.

If one were to see the swastika on a copy of old Kipling, without doing a little research, one would quickly condemn Kipling as an author based on this one image. We bring our own worldview and understanding to bear on what we see and read. So we easily misunderstand. In a sense, then, we misread.

This is what Lewis is telling us can happen with words and language. We can bring a modern understanding to a word and misunderstand, sometimes with disastrous results. But also, we can see how words (and symbols) can be snatched and supplied with tactical definitions to support the ends of certain groups and ideologies. We have to be able to see through the ways words are being co-opted for purposes of propaganda, manipulation, and control. We have to take the time to look at the history of language, as Lewis suggests, so we don't misread or misunderstand and so condemn or ostracize. We need to resolve, insofar as it lies within our capability, not to participate in the death of language. This requires an awareness of how we are currently using language. We are less likely to do this kind of painstaking work, but it won't stop us from agreeing with Lewis that we should do it if we are to read and speak and understand well.

Studies in Words has implications for our faith as well. God is revealed to us—at least partly—through the Scriptures. And what are Scriptures? Essentially *writings*. Words. And how often do we bring our own worldview to bear on a passage of Scripture without taking the time to explore the actual meaning? Specious interpretations may abound. If there was ever a text where erroneous interpretations are legion, even among biblical scholars, this must be it. How often do we read Scriptures with complete disregard for the historical and cultural traditions contained therein? And how many of us have knowledge of the constructs of oral versus print culture and what that must mean for interpretation of this text? Not to mention the myriad ways that the text has been twisted to serve certain ends. One recalls Thomas Jefferson reading the New Testament with scissors in hand. Gaining a knowledge of these things is vital to interpretation. In his own thinking about this issue Lewis writes:

> Heaven is, by definition, outside our experience, but all intelligible descriptions must be of things within our experience. The scriptural picture of heaven is therefore just as symbolical as the picture which our desire, unaided, invents for itself; heaven is not really full of jewelry any more than it is really the beauty of Nature, or a fine piece of music. The difference is that the scriptural imagery has authority. It comes to us from writers who were closer to God than we, and it has stood the test of Christian experience down the centuries. The natural appeal of this authoritative imagery is to me, at first, very small. At first

sight it chills, rather than awakes, my desire. And that is just what I ought to expect. If Christianity could tell me no more of the far-off land than my own temperament led me to surmise already, then Christianity would be no higher than myself. If it has more to give me, I must expect it to be less immediately attractive than "my own stuff." Sophocles at first seems dull and cold to the boy who has only reached Shelley. If our religion is something objective, then we must never avert our eyes from those elements in it which seem puzzling or repellent; for it will be precisely the puzzling or the repellent which conceals what we do not yet know and need to know.[218]

Here is the implicit call for additional research, for taking the time to understand what the ancient writers meant, for not trusting in our own worldview or hermeneutic. And here, if we are to grow more deeply in our faith, we must make the effort to understand what we currently do not know. We must take the time to study, to examine word meanings in original languages, to understand the context and the historical milieu in which a text was written. It seems to me that an increasingly accurate knowledge of God's work in history through this kind of understanding is of vital interest to the Christian. Only then will we have the opportunity to penetrate to a deeper truth or correct a potentially disastrous error. And Lewis gives us the tools to begin this difficult but necessary work.

---

218   Lewis, *The Weight of Glory*, "The Weight of Glory" (New York: Simon & Schuster, 1996), 30–31.

Chapter 6

Becoming a Thousand Men

An Experiment in Criticism

An Experiment in Criticism was written to turn the dominant literary criticism of Lewis's day on its head. This criticism, Lewis writes, was usually employed in judging the content of books as either good or bad. By extension, it could be inferred that someone who read a book judged as good by the critics must have had good taste, and those that read a book judged as bad by the critics must have had bad taste.

But Lewis wondered if a better form of criticism would be possible if a good book could be defined as one that is read in one way and a bad book as one that is read in another way.[219] To this end he divided readers into

219 Lewis, *An Experiment in Criticism* (New York: Cambridge University Press, 2008), 1.

two categories: the many and the few. He wanted to understand what made for a full reading experience. He sought an enlargement of his being through reading rightly. And it is the nature of this enlargement that we ultimately want to understand.

On Reading for the Many

Lewis writes that the many, or the unliterary, use art for their own ends; if it can't be used, it is meaningless. This is not a bad response, just not a full one, he notes. Yet it is this presence of a full response that separates the many from the few. The many never read any work twice, and in fact reading isn't valued much at all. They aren't changed by what they read, nor do they think about it. And they never read anything that isn't narrative with swift moving action.[220] Everything must be easily recognizable for the many. They don't want to work or use their imagination, and thus, everything must be spelled out. This leads them to writing that is full of cliché, because it is imperative that things should be easily recognizable. Words must act as hieroglyphs and release stereotyped reactions. For example, to denote fear, one would write "his blood ran cold."[221]

Lewis also notes that the many have no ears.[222] That is, they read by eye and don't observe the artistry or style. Part of this lack of appreciation has to do with certain mindsets that destroy appreciation and lead to poor reading. He outlines five different mindsets.

First is economic necessity or overwork. Lewis is thinking here of overworked literary critics who must read for their job or scholars who must regularly publish and be seen to say something new about their field or lose their jobs. Second is the reader as status seeker. This is the individual swayed by trends, reading only the

---

220 Lewis, *An Experiment in Criticism*, 2.
221 Lewis, *An Experiment in Criticism*, 33.
222 Lewis, *An Experiment in Criticism*, 29.

"approved works" that are current or in vogue or are endorsed by some celebrity. Lewis writes that in a household with this mindset, often the only true literary experience taking place is the small boy upstairs reading *Treasure Island* under the covers at night with a flashlight. Third is the devotee of culture. This individual reads to improve himself. Lewis notes that his motivations may be good, but he may not actually be a true lover of literature. Fourth are the arbiters of what is good to read, what Lewis calls the vigilant school of critics. In our own day we might think of Mortimer Adler's *How to Read a Book* or Harold Bloom's *How to Read and Why* as artifacts of this vigilant school.

Finally, there is the mindset of reading as a meritorious activity, often the result of one's upbringing.[223] We are made to feel that we should be reading certain works. Many of us have had this kind of checklist mentality. If we read a book, we check it off our list, even though much of the time we only have a dim notion of what we actually read. Alan Jacobs, formerly of Wheaton College in Illinois, used to teach a seminar class in which the focus of the class was to study the ways we read, and during it he recommended the idea of reading at whim. This is some of the best reading advice one can receive. Jacobs (now of Baylor University) would likely be a proponent of Lewis's idea of what constitutes good reading. It is one that advocates reading for pleasure and joy and to receive something.

In his book *The Pleasures of Reading in an Age of Distraction* Jacobs writes that he had received a number of requests from people for a list of books that they should read. While it may be a bit overstated, this is his response:

> So this is what I say to my petitioners: for heaven's sake, don't turn reading into the intellectual equivalent of eating organic greens, or (shifting the metaphor slightly) some fearfully

223 Lewis, *An Experiment in Criticism*, 6–10.

disciplined appointment with an elliptical trainer of the mind in which you count words or pages the way some people fix their attention on the "calories burned" readout—some assiduous and taxing exercise that allows you to look back on your conquest of *Middlemarch* with grim satisfaction. How depressing. This kind of thing is not reading at all, but what C. S. Lewis called "social and ethical hygiene."[224]

The Lewis reference here is to the school of vigilant critics and the manner in which they do literary criticism. Each of these mindsets is a deterrent to appreciation and receptiveness and leads to poor reading.

But Lewis is careful to clarify his points. He notes that we must not equate the many with the rabble and so imply a moral judgment. We must not play the cultural snob as these are not rigid categories. People can move between the two classes or appreciate different arts in different ways.[225]

On Reading for the Few

The few, or the literary, Lewis writes, are the ones who have a full literary experience. There is a loss of self in their process of reading. They desire silence and leisure in which to pursue their reading habit and will read a single work multiple times. Reading is believed to change one's consciousness. And they recall and converse about literature with others. A work is accepted for itself, not for what it can do. These readers value an absorption of the mind. They approach the work wholeheartedly. That is, they read in the same spirit that the author wrote. They need a minimum amount of detail. And they have what Lewis calls the fertile imagination, which can build in a moment from bare facts. They are receptive and their minds are open without preconceptions.[226]

---

224   Alan Jacobs, *The Pleasures of Reading in an Age of Distraction* (New York: Oxford University Press, 2011), 17.
225   Lewis, *An Experiment in Criticism*, 5–6.
226   Lewis, *An Experiment in Criticism*, 2–3.

Lewis writes elsewhere that there are two activities of the imagination, the free and the servile. The free activity is the daydream from which the self is absent. The servile activity is the daydream that is pure self-aggrandizement. It sees the self as the hero of every story. Lewis himself gave examples of his own free imagination: the imaginary village of mice called Snugtown, the unknown room in a house that he was always waiting to discover and a garden that existed partly in the west and partly in the past. The primary point is that these imaginings are simply loved for what they are.[227]

He goes on to say that this kind of real literary appreciation involves both a negative and positive process. On the negative side, these readers must strip out subjectivity, lay aside their preconceptions, interests and associations, and surrender the self to the narrative. On the positive side readers must look to see what is there and wait for something to be done to them. That is, they must receive something from the work. And Lewis writes that this is one of the primary differences between the many and the few. The many use literature and the few receive it.[228]

Another element valued by the few are those stories that contain an extra-literary quality. They have an effect on us that is unique. Lewis defines this quality as mythic. He notes that this does not have to mean stories related to traditional myths. We may even read these and not have such a mythic response. But by this term he means a story with certain characteristics.

A mythic narrative strikes deeply, independent of the telling of it. Any version will still have the same effect on us. There is a sort of inevitability about the tale; it almost exists for us as an object of permanent contemplation. Our human sympathy is at a minimum, so we don't project ourselves into it; we are exercising the free activity of the imagination. And these tales often deal with

227   Lewis, *Selected Literary Essays*, "Psycho-Analysis and Literary Criticism" (New York: Cambridge University Press, 1969), 290.
228   Lewis, *An Experiment in Criticism*, 18–19.

the fantastic. They give us an experience that is grave and awe-inspiring. Lewis writes that we give to these stories the "lasting allegiance of the imagination."[229]

He is careful here to make a distinction about the word "fantastic," or "fantasy." The word in its literary definition means a narrative that deals with impossibles and preternaturals: things beyond the normal and natural. He writes that "fantasy" can be a psychological term as well, with three definitions. The first definition is any imaginative construction that a person takes to be literal reality. Thus it becomes delusion. Second is any imaginative construction that is not mistaken for reality, but is entertained incessantly. When this type of imagining is indulged in long enough, reality becomes insipid by comparison. Lewis calls this morbid castle-building. Third is any person who uses an imaginative construction briefly or as a temporary reverie, but actively lives in reality. This is normal castle-building. Normal castle-building itself can be further subdivided into egoistic and disinterested. These correspond to the servile and free activities of the imagination that we discussed earlier. The more one reads, Lewis notes, as an egoistic castle-builder, the more a superficial realism will be demanded and the less the truly fantastic is liked.[230]

Lewis makes another distinction about the term "realism." He writes that there are two types of realism. First is realism of presentation. This type of literary description brings something close. It is palpable and vivid, with sharply imagined detail. It utilizes the five senses and requires a certain suspension of disbelief. Second is realism of content. This is description that is probable or true to life but contains little or no detail and requires no suspension of disbelief. Lewis writes that up until the present, most literature was written with realism of presentation. It dealt with the fantastic in some way because it was only the

229   Lewis, *An Experiment in Criticism*, 43–44.
230   Lewis, *An Experiment in Criticism*, 50–52.

exceptional event that merited a story. Similarly, in conversation, we tend to relate the fantastic or strange stories, not what is dull or common.[231]

Lewis acknowledges that there may be arguments against fairy tales or fantasy. The first charge is that they merely deceive. They do not tell the truth about reality. Second, they may be charged with being escapist. This often coincides with a charge of childishness. Lewis notes that all reading is an escape, but the important point to consider is, an escape to what? It may be that we escape into negative imaginings like egoistic castle-building. Or perhaps we are engaged in disinterested castle-building, using the free activity of the imagination. The taste for fantasy is normal, Lewis reassures us, but atrophied in adults. Thus, he calls for an escapism rightly understood. He states that we must lose our chronological snobbery, that is, we must not believe that the literature or popular genres of our own age or time are the only ones that have something to offer us and that other ages or literary genres are backward. We must be open to learning from the art and literature of the past, not only the distant past, but even our own past childhood when the taste for fantasy was in full flower.[232]

How the Few Misread

We have considered how the few read well, but we must now turn to how they also misread. Lewis suggests that this misreading often stems from a confusion between art and life. Art is made of the stuff of life; it is selected, isolated and picked from here and there to suit the artist's purpose. We can't, therefore, fall into the trap of confusing art with life, yet we often do.[233]

Fixating on psychological truths or reflections that come out of a work, rather than its artistry, is one way the few misread. Lewis

---

231 Lewis, *An Experiment in Criticism*, 57–62.
232 Lewis, *An Experiment in Criticism*, 67–71.
233 Lewis, *An Experiment in Criticism*, 74–78.

writes that this is using the work rather than receiving it and we miss out on what the artist has made for us. And any reflections we make come from us, not from the artist. The work itself, as a thing made, is important to Lewis because it serves as a guard against simply using a work as a mouthpiece for what we want it to say. He notes that a work of art is really two things: a thing said, and a thing made. The *logos*, or the thing said, deals with the meaning, the events and the plot, as well as opinions and emotions. The *poiema*, or the thing made, refers to the "is-ness" of the work of art, its being. Principles of design, contrast, balance, shape, and the organization of words that produces what Lewis calls a patterned experience are examples of *poiema*.[234] He writes elsewhere—in *A Preface to Paradise Lost*—that we must love a work for itself, as the man writing the love sonnet not only loves the beloved, but also the sonnet.[235] That is, we must love the art, the craft, the builded thing that a particular work is. When we don't acknowledge this as a fundamental part of the literary experience and look only to see what the work can give us, we misread. Ignoring the *poiema* of a work and focusing only on criticism that gives us what we want ultimately leads us to ourselves. Lewis writes that "One of the chief operations of art is to remove our gaze from that mirrored face, to deliver us from that solitude."[236]

Lewis desires us to focus on what the work can do *to* us, rather than what we can get out of it. He suggests that we ought to enter fully into the attitudes and opinions and experiences of other people rather than being concerned with altering our own opinions:

> To enjoy our full humanity we ought, so far as is possible, to contain within us potentially at all times, and on occasion to actualize, all the modes of feeling and thinking through which

234 Lewis, *An Experiment in Criticism*, 82.
235 Lewis, *A Preface to Paradise Lost*, 3.
236 Lewis, *An Experiment in Criticism*, 85.

man has passed. You must, so far as in you lies, become an Achaean chief while reading Homer, a medieval knight while reading Malory, and an Eighteenth-Century Londoner while reading Johnson. Only then will you be able to judge the work "in the same spirit that its author writ" and to avoid chimerical criticism.[237]

This theme surfaces again and again in Lewis. He is arguing for a full experience, the success of which depends upon our ability to get ourselves out of the way and allow the art to work on us. We must be willing to let go of analysis, preconceptions, and our general worldview and simply bask in the work without the attempt to get anything from it. In this way, we become receivers of literature rather than users. Again, he writes:

We want to know—therefore, as far as may be, we want to live through for ourselves—the experience of men long dead. What a poem may "mean" to moderns, and to them only, however delightful, is from this point of view merely a stain on the lens. We must clean the lens and remove the stain so that the real past can be seen better.[238]

Lewis's Method of Literary Criticism

So far, we have examined how the two categories of readers read. Recall that Lewis is attempting to subvert the current criticism of his day. This criticism is employed to judge books as good or bad. Therefore, as we've mentioned previously, it follows that someone who reads a book judged as good by the critics must have good taste, and those that read a book judged as bad by the critics must have bad taste.

---

237   Lewis, *A Preface to Paradise Lost*, 63.
238   Lewis, *Studies in Medieval and Renaissance Literature*, "De Audiendis Poetis" (New York: Cambridge University Press, 2007), 2.

But for Lewis, this was too simplistic. He wanted to see if there was a better way to think about how people experience literature. He has made it clear that the method of judging is not feasible in understanding what makes a good book good or a bad one bad. Instead, he set out to discover how far it would be possible to reverse this process and judge literature by the way people read it.

Lewis's rationale for reading and doing criticism in this manner is, first of all, that it fixes our attention on reading rather than on how a book may be valued by critics. The real value of literature, he writes, is only found where good readers read, in the reading act itself. We must not be distracted by abstractions about what makes a book good or bad.[239] Second, Lewis's rationale puts our feet on solid ground. The prevailing views of the literary world on some particular author or work will wax and wane, and generally behave in a mercurial fashion. If we observe how people read, we are better able to judge what they read.[240] Third, it helps us to banish social and intellectual snobbery. We may find certain books distasteful and be tempted to regard them as bad works, but Lewis suggests that if even one person had found delight in these books, we should remain silent and not dare to judge them as bad.[241]

Lewis objected to the literary criticism of his day largely because it was evaluative; critics pushed their judgments on others. But he calls for critics who can get themselves out of the way and let readers decide. They are merely to describe the book as it is.[242] Criticism, he states, becomes one-sided when it focuses on the *logos* of a work, or the thing said. This one-sided approach is likened by Lewis to criticizing the lens after looking at it, rather than through it.[243] To have a full experience, we must do both kinds of looking. This idea is further developed in his essay "Meditation in a Toolshed," where he describes an experience he had while standing in a toolshed.

239 Lewis, *An Experiment in Criticism*, 104.
240 Lewis, *An Experiment in Criticism*, 105.
241 Lewis, *An Experiment in Criticism*, 108.
242 Lewis, *An Experiment in Criticism*, 120.
243 Lewis, *An Experiment in Criticism*, 36.

In the darkness, he noticed a beam of sunlight shining through a gap in the shed doors. As he looked at the beam, he could see the dust motes dancing in it. But as he bent down and looked along the beam, he was able to see tree leaves in the breeze outside and beyond that, the sun.[244]

Why This Book Is Important

An Experiment in Criticism is about how one may engage in good or poor reading. But for Lewis, the reading experience ultimately pointed to something more, to things that certainly should be of vital interest to the Christian. He writes in his essay "On Stories" about how in a life of successive moments we are always searching for something that is non-successive, some moment where we will have finally arrived, or connected, or self-actualized.[245] We all do this. The "grass is greener" mentality is a deep habit of the contemporary mind. We think that if we can just find that right person, make that certain amount of money, live in that other location, have that particular opportunity, then we will have reached the apotheosis of human longing.

But in fact, we never do arrive. When we get to whatever place we thought was going to give us that feeling we so desired, we realize that it is just as unattainable as ever. In *The Weight of Glory* Lewis writes:

> We want something else which can hardly be put into words—to be united with the beauty we see, to pass into it, to receive it into ourselves, to bathe in it, to become part of it. That is why we have peopled air and earth and water with gods and goddesses and nymphs and elves—that, though we cannot, yet these projections can enjoy in themselves that beauty, grace and power of which

244 Lewis, *God in the Dock*, "Meditation in a Toolshed" (Grand Rapids, MI: Eerdmans, 1970), 212–15.
245 Lewis, *Of Other Worlds*, "On Stories" (New York: Harcourt Brace Jovanovich, 1966), 20–21.

Nature is the image. . . . At present we are on the outside of the world, the wrong side of the door. . . . But all the leaves of the New Testament are rustling with the rumour that it will not always be so. Some day, God willing, we shall get in.[246]

We all have longings to be united with we know not what; perhaps it was what Lewis called *sehnsucht*, a longing akin to joy. But he notes that in literature, we can sometimes get close to an experience of these non-successive moments.[247] And it is the kind of reading practiced by the few that could take us there. This is perhaps why Lewis is so eager for us to think about how we read rather than what we read. If we can fully enter into a text, we have a greater chance to get close to these experiences of completion or unity.

In his essay "Myth Became Fact" he writes of one of the tragic human dilemmas: "This is our dilemma," he states, "either to taste and not to know or to know and not to taste—or, more strictly, to lack one kind of knowledge because we are in an experience or to lack another kind because we are outside it."[248] We cannot both experience something and think about it at the same time. When we are doing either, we are by necessity shutting the other out.

For Lewis, myth was a partial solution to this tragic dilemma. He notes that when we enjoy a great myth, we can almost experience as concrete what would otherwise only be an abstraction. Myths can make abstract principles imaginable. While you are reading a myth, you are not thinking about what it means, but it turns out that when we bask in the story, what we are experiencing is an abstract principle. If you stop to think about it, you are back in the world of abstraction and out of the experience. Nevertheless, in Lewis's mind, myth helped connect these two ways of seeing.[249] Here again, we see the longing for a unity, for some kind of reconciliation, even if only

246   Lewis, *The Weight of Glory*, 37.
247   Lewis, *Of Other Worlds*, 21.
248   Lewis, *God in the Dock*, "Myth Became Fact," 65.
249   Lewis, *God in the Dock*, 66.

partial, that will give us an approximation of closeness to the non-successive for which we all long.

Another important reason to read fully, engaging in primary literary experience, is that it is vital to culture. Yet evaluative criticism has all but killed this kind of response. The individual response to literature is becoming rarer and this state of affairs is dangerous, Lewis notes. His solution? Banish all evaluative criticism that would steal away the joy of a full reading experience.[250] But in our current culture, where very few are actively reading, what place can literary criticism have? This seems to be a moot point.

Unfortunately for us, we live in an age that increasingly disvalues the act of reading, where the proliferation of screen technologies has nearly eradicated any interest in or even need for literature and reading. We are told what to think and what is important by the tech companies producing the myriad devices that we seem to find necessary in order to exist. We follow along, unquestioning, accepting every new "advance" as inevitable and good. This is destroying our ability to have a unique literary response. Lewis's sense of urgency seems to suggest that reading in this way must give us something unique, some experience we cannot get anywhere else, certainly not through our digital devices.

Lewis intimates that part of what makes this experience unique is the importance of others' voices and viewpoints. First, we need to listen to others' voices because we ourselves do not contain all knowledge and experience. In reading, we seek an enlargement of our being; we want to be more than ourselves. He states that we demand windows; this gets us out of ourselves, corrects provincialism in our point of view, and heals loneliness. We often exist in a narrow prison of self. He writes: "My own eyes are not enough for me, I will see through those of others. Reality, even seen through the eyes of many, is not enough. I will see what others have invented. Even the eyes of all humanity are not enough. I regret

250   Lewis, *An Experiment in Criticism*, 129.

that the brutes cannot write books. Very gladly would I learn what face things present to a mouse or a bee; more gladly still would I perceive the olfactory world charged with all the information and emotion it carries for a dog."[251]

In a culture that values information over wisdom, activity, and busyness and digital noise over silence and contemplation, where information is valued more than transformation, our windows have become darkened—worse yet, we no longer care to look out of these windows, or even realize that there are windows out of which to look.

We are much less apt to read a book now than we were fifty years ago. In some ways, reading the way Lewis describes it is now an elegiac activity, only attainable by those who have clung tenaciously to old habits and skills. And the question persists, how likely is it that we have the ability to develop the skills required for this kind of literary experience—skills that were once a birthright, but have steadily diminished as print culture lost ascendency to digital culture? Author and social critic Sven Birkerts writes that contemplation is the point of thinking. This requires solitude, time-as-duration and a lingering among intimations and suppositions.[252] These are seemingly long-lost skills in the current cultural climate, but necessary to Lewis's way of reading fully. So part of our task— if we choose to believe what he suggests, that reading gives us an experience that we can't quite get anywhere else—will be to recover a relationship with print and the disciplines attendant on that recovery that will allow us to read well and so experience a work more fully.

Without a full reading experience it is too easy to fall back into self-referentialism and perceive the world only through our eyes, through the narrow prison of self. Instead of looking out of the prison bars, we sink back on the straw in the darkest corner. The

251 Lewis, *An Experiment in Criticism*, 140.
252 Sven Birkerts, *Changing the Subject* (Minneapolis: Graywolf Press, 2015), 93.

exigencies of reading are part of the solution. It is the urgency we must have to wake up, to see the world rightly, to see it from other viewpoints. For Lewis, this was clearly one of the most important outcomes of good reading. When our horizons are widened, we approach life and relationships with more understanding, thoughtfulness and compassion and are able to identify with others in new ways. Lewis notes that all reality is iconoclastic. Reading helps break down barriers of blindness and get a clearer bearing on the truth of reality.

This waking up to reality, to seeing the world as it really is, is part of a beneficial iconoclasm. Lewis notes this about the writing of George MacDonald: "The quality that had enchanted me in his imaginative works turned out to be the quality of the real universe, the divine, magical, terrifying and ecstatic reality in which we all live."[253] In a culture that works unceasingly to keep us blinded to the realities around us, this is vital for the Christian. We need to be alert to the world that is charged with the grandeur of God, to see it truly and clearly. This takes an effort of what Lewis terms the "satisfied imagination,"[254] the ability to re-enchant the familiar and find pleasure in the mundane such that everything we see becomes a channel through which we worship our creator.

In *Letters to Malcolm*, Lewis outlines four obstacles that prevent us from perceiving these pleasures. The first is simple inattention. We are unaware, and the plethora of distractions in our society doesn't help to hone our awareness. The second is the wrong kind of attention. We could imagine that the pleasure is simply taking place within us and ignore "the smell of Deity that hangs about it." For example, Lewis notes, we might hear just a roar, rather than the roaring of the wind. A third is greed, desiring the pleasure again and again. The fourth is the conceited attitude that not everyone is privileged to have the understanding we have been vouchsafed.

---

253 Lewis, ed. *George MacDonald* (New York: HarperCollins, 2001), xxxviii.
254 Lewis, *The Discarded Image* (New York: Cambridge University Press, 1974), 203.

It is a position of superiority. The ability to recognize God in our pleasures and mundanities is a discipline, but for Lewis, as it succeeds, it gives him bearings on what he calls the bright blur, or God. As we learn to avoid these obstacles to identifying pleasures and develop an awareness toward them, the blur becomes brighter and clearer.[255]

Reading at the level Lewis advocates is a yearning for connection and clarity, to imagine oneself living many lives, seeing through many eyes the many ways the world can be apprehended. It is a way to engage in beneficial iconoclasm, in breaking down those barriers of blindness that keep our hearts and minds fettered. This kind of reading helps us awaken from the lethargy of self-delusion. G. K. Chesterton noted that "if you look at a thing 999 times, you are perfectly safe. If you look at it for the 1000th time, you are in frightful danger of seeing it for the first time."[256] This is what the eyes of others can give us, where we finally see beyond ourselves, the windows are opened, the light streams in, and our view of the world clarifies and expands.

255 Lewis, *Letters to Malcolm: Chiefly on Prayer* (New York: Harcourt, Brace & World, Inc., 1964), 90–91.
256 G. K. Chesterton, *The Napoleon of Notting Hill* in *The Collected Works of G.K. Chesterton, Vol.* 6 (San Francisco: Ignatius Press, 1991), 227.

Chapter 7

The Heavens Declare the Glory

The Discarded Image

The Discarded Image was published in 1964. It was one of Lewis's final books before he passed away in November of 1963. It contains what were originally the Prolegomena to the Study of Medieval and Renaissance Literature lectures for students at Oxford, delivered in 1932, and then continues with various additions over the following years. Lewis writes that his purpose in collecting these lectures into a book was to facilitate a more accurate reading of the imaginative literature written during the medieval period. To this end he provides us with a picture of the medieval model or worldview, including its cosmology, and how this worldview influenced the artistic output of the period. He likens it to a map that one consults before traveling through a specific region. The map serves to correct any mistakes that might be made in bringing a modern conception to bear on old texts and so misreading them.[257]

Background to the Model

The popular impression of the medieval age isn't accurate, writes Lewis. Our cultural mythologies see this era as one of romance and ballads, of knights in armor and damsels in distress. But the real temper of this age is classical, not romantic. It is an age characterized by formal structures, logic, order, unity, and proportion.[258]

Medieval thought arose from two primary sources. First, from a love of system. The medievals were codifiers and organizers. They concerned themselves with making distinctions, tabulations, definitions, sorting out, tidying up. They were incredibly systematic. Lewis's metaphor for this preoccupation with codification is the card indexing system, for those of us who are old enough to remember it. The characteristic artistic examples of this period would be Dante's *Divine Comedy*, the *Summa Theologica* of Thomas Aquinas, Salisbury Cathedral, and the medieval model itself.

The second source from which medieval thought arose was books. It was a bookish-minded culture, yet the medievals had lost most of their books. The ones that remained or were passed down were an eclectic mix of Judaic, pagan, Platonic, Aristotelian, Stoical, primitive, Christian, and Patristic. Medieval scholars were extremely credulous and found it difficult to disbelieve anything written in a book.[259]

Because of this love of system and credulity toward texts, medieval thought tended toward the syncretistic and hierarchical. This was because they had inherited so few and such a heterogeneous

---

257 Lewis, *The Discarded Image* (New York: Cambridge University Press, 1974), vii.
258 Lewis, *Studies in Medieval and Renaissance Literature*, "Imagination and Thought in the Middle Ages" (New York: Cambridge University Press, 2007), 44.
259 Lewis, *The Discarded Image*, 10–11.

assortment of texts, and because of this credulity, any contradictions between texts had to be harmonized. Everything was linked to everything else. This is why we see so many different elements jumbled together in medieval works of art. It is also why we should not expect the medieval model to be specifically Christian.[260]

Medieval people were aware of the fact that all models must, in the end, be provisional. All theories should, therefore, save the appearances (account for all the observable data). A caveat developed by William of Occam was appended to this theory, stating that not only should all theories save the appearances, they should do so with the fewest possible assumptions. This is commonly known as Occam's Razor.[261]

Not only were all models provisional, they were also metaphorical, Lewis writes. For example, the medievals understood gravity as what they called "kindly enclyning." If a stone is dropped, it falls to the ground because it wants to return to its home, its native environment. Our current understanding of gravity as a law or a force of attraction between two objects is no less metaphorical. However, the metaphor we choose to explain certain phenomena makes a difference to us on the emotional and imaginative level.[262] The medievals saw a universe packed with beauty and significance. A modern sensibility tends to see the universe in terms of fear: as an infinite, empty void.

Sources from Which the Model was Derived

The classical period (roughly 50 BC to AD 125) provided contributions to this medieval temper from the works of (among others) Cicero, Lucan, and Apuleius. Cicero contributed to the understanding of the heavens: the *stellatum* or region of fixed stars, the influence of the planets and the moon as a boundary between

260 Lewis, *The Discarded Image*, 11.
261 Lewis, *The Discarded Image*, 15–16.
262 Lewis, *The Discarded Image*, 92–94.

the earth and heavens (actually borrowed from Aristotle). Lucan contributed to an understanding of what lies between the earth and this boundary of the moon. Apuleius brought the idea of the intermediary (borrowed from Plato) which suggests that any two things need a third to bridge them. This idea then engenders the medieval notion of the triad, which we will examine in due course. Another contribution from Apuleius is the idea of plenitude, a full exploitation of the universe in the sense of packing it full of significance.[263]

Lewis suggests that it was the seminal period (AD 205 to 533) that ushered in the characteristic medieval frame of mind. It saw contributions from both Christian and pagan writers, two groups that had much closer affinities in thought and belief than is generally acknowledged. For example, both groups were characterized by monotheism, intellectual rigor, belief in the supernatural, and an ascetic and mystical temper. The belief that the pagans were sensualists and the Christians ascetics is an error, Lewis writes.[264]

Plato and subsequent commentaries on Plato contributed heavily to this period. Lewis details four main ones: Chalcidius, Macrobius, Pseudo-Dionysius, and Boethius. Chalcidius was a translator of Plato's *Timaeus*, an account of cosmology that heavily influenced the medieval model. He also further developed the triadic ideas of Apuleius. Macrobius, a pagan author, brought neo-Platonism to the model through a commentary on Cicero's *Republic*, and Pseudo-Dionysius brought a robust understanding of angelology. But for Lewis, Boethius was by far the most influential author of this period due to the contributions from his work *The Consolation of Philosophy*.[265]

All of these influences show the varied texts that medieval people had at their disposal to create the model of the earth and

263 Lewis, *The Discarded Image*, 22–24.
264 Lewis, *The Discarded Image*, 46–47.
265 Lewis, *The Discarded Image*, 45–91.

heavens and humanity's relation to them. As we have previously mentioned, the model was a great syncretistic work, or blending of all these sources from which medieval people could derive endless delight and by means of which their minds were always carried back to the source of all delight: God.

The Model

Lewis writes that "the human imagination has seldom had before it an object so sublimely ordered as the medieval cosmos."[266] It is to this ordering of the heavens that we now turn, to a brief overview of the main structure of the model. An understanding of it is essential to an understanding of Lewis himself, his literary preoccupations, and his fiction.

To begin, we must remember that the medieval universe was Ptolemaic and thus geocentric. It was unimaginably large, yet finite. Lewis writes that we should see it in terms of height rather than distance, like looking up at a towering building. It was a universe to look into rather than out on.[267]

The moon was the line of demarcation between the earth and the heavens. Everything above the region of the moon was thought to be immutable, non-contingent and incorruptible. Everything below the region of the moon, including the earth and its inhabitants, was thought to be mutable, contingent, subject to change and decay.[268]

The heavens consisted of seven planets, ranging upwards into unfathomable distance beginning with the moon and then on to Mercury, Venus, the sun, Mars, Jupiter, and Saturn. Above the planets were the stellatum or region of fixed stars, and above this the Primum Mobile or first mover. It was the outermost sphere that caused the movements of all the planets below it. Above this was the Empyrean, containing God or the divine substance.

266 Lewis, *The Discarded Image*, 121.
267 Lewis, *The Discarded Image*, 99.
268 Lewis, *The Discarded Image*, 108.

Lewis suggests that the medievals maintained an animistic conception of the heavens. Each sphere or planet was associated with an intelligence, a conscious and intellectual being who energized the planet into motion.[269] All movement in this universe began with a love for God. To the Greeks, the circle was the symbol of perfection, and therefore a sphere could most closely approximate its love for God by turning in a circle. But it could only do so by receiving knowledge of God from the planet directly above it. Thus, each planet passed on its knowledge of God to the planet below it, and in this we see the great medieval principle of devolution. As we move downward through the heavens toward the earth, all power and speed are attenuated. Movement is slower and impulse weaker, because the knowledge of God is now at many removes.[270]

Planets were also thought to have influence on the earth. For example, writes Lewis, each planet was associated with a particular metal: the sun with gold, the moon with silver and so on. The influence of each planet, reaching the earth, produced its particular metal in the ground. But the planets also influenced human psychology. The moon produced madness, Jupiter produced joviality and so forth. This led to a sort of astrological determinism in which it was felt that one didn't really have free will.[271]

The heavens were not dark as we know them to be. To the medieval mind, they were lighted. The darkness of night was simply thought to be the cone of earth's shadow. And not only were the heavens lighted, but they were also full of sound. The heavens swelled with a music that, paradoxically, having always been heard, could not be heard at all. One could liken this to electricity, whose ambient hum remains unheard until the power goes out and we sense a deeper silence. Until it is gone, we do not know it is there.[272]

269 Lewis, *The Discarded Image*, 115.
270 Lewis, *Studies in Medieval and Renaissance Literature*, "Imagination and Thought in the Middle Ages," 51–58.
271 Lewis, *The Discarded Image*, 105–9.
272 Lewis, *Studies in Medieval and Renaissance Literature*, 52.

All of this order of the heavens was seen as a dance of high pageantry, Lewis writes. It is as if we on the earth are outside of the city or castle wall, looking in and longing to take part. He likens it to animals staring at the fires of an encampment they cannot enter or rustics gazing into the distance at a city. It is a yearning to take part in a perfect, ordered, reiterated dance. What is this dance? Simply the yearning to approximate God.[273] And those on earth, below the boundary of the moon, existed in the realm of contingence and decay. Here, everything was subject to randomness and disorder. Fortune, the intelligence associated with earth, was responsible for the rise and fall of empires. Because it was the realm of contingence, everything happened at Fortune's whim.[274]

Earth itself was composed of four elements: earth, air, fire, water. The water surrounded the earth. The air was divided into an upper and lower region, inhabited by creatures called daemons, which Plato described as creatures of a middle nature between gods and men. It was through the daemons that humans could have access to the gods. This created a triadic relationship in which the daemon acted as the medium between the planet as agent and man as patient. This perfectly illustrates the great medieval idea of the triad, first contributed by Apuleius, by which this universe was constructed and in which it was repeated again and again. Above the air, but below the boundary of the moon, was the region of fire. One must not think of this as fire in the ordinary sense of flames, but as pure, unadulterated fire, invisible and transparent.[275]

From earth, we pass to the human, and specifically to the medieval understanding of the human soul. The soul was seen to be tripartite, consisting of rational, sensitive, and vegetable components. The rational helped one to grasp intelligible truth as well as enable him to reason. The sensitive was comprised of the ten senses or wits.

273   Lewis, *Studies in Medieval and Renaissance Literature*, 59–60.
274   Lewis, *The Discarded Image*, 139–40.
275   Lewis, *The Discarded Image*, 96.

These were further subdivided into the inward and outward. The inward senses included memory, estimation, imagination, phantasy, and common wit. The outward senses included sight, hearing, taste, touch, and smell. The vegetable component of the soul was responsible for all of the unconscious processes that go on in our bodies. This understanding of the soul is yet another illustration of the triadic nature of the medieval worldview.[276]

A final important concept was the understanding of the human past. History was meant to do three things: entertain the imagination, gratify curiosity, and discharge a debt owed to ancestors. Medieval people felt a responsibility to pass on the great stories of the past. They didn't question the veracity of these stories, but merely accepted them as true. Lewis states that the modern passion for the assertion of facts would have destroyed the imaginative impact of medieval historiography. It was this understanding that led them to humility in the face of history.[277] Lewis explains:

> Historically as well as cosmically, medieval man stood at the foot
> of a stairway; looking up he felt delight. The backward, like the
> upward, glance, exhilarated him with a majestic spectacle, and
> humility was rewarded with the pleasures of admiration. . . . One
> had one's place, however modest, in a great succession; one need
> neither be proud nor lonely.[278]

Influence of the Model Then and Now

Lewis writes of the medieval cosmology that "Other ages have not had a Model so universally accepted as theirs, so imaginable, and so satisfying to the imagination." It had an especially great influence on the arts of the time. In fact, the role of the arts was to depict elements of the model. Artists loved these things simply for

276   Lewis, *The Discarded Image*, 152–64.
277   Lewis, *The Discarded Image*, 174–84.
278   Lewis, *The Discarded Image*, 185.

themselves. To them, everything was more interesting if it carried the mind back to the model.[279] To this end, medieval artists believed in restating what already existed. This resulted in a stodginess of expression that was the characteristic vice of medieval art, but particularly of its literature. However, Lewis writes, its virtue was an absence of strain. The stories almost tell themselves. Artists were absorbed in their subject matter. They didn't create new works. The goal was simply to hand on the great stories of the past. They possessed the realizing imagination—that is, they were able to make others see what they saw.[280]

Another influence of the model is that it created significance. The model had a built-in significance. Not only was it a manifestation of the wisdom and goodness that created it, but its highly imaginable components also helped frame a richer understanding of the heavens and one's place in the scheme of things. It led the mind to worship in a way that our modern understanding of the heavens does not. Lewis also explains how this is in direct opposition to the modern sensibility that thinks it can't know the significance of reality at all.[281]

Finally, the model inspired humility. Medieval authors were not caught up in self-aggrandizement. They would have felt this to be an admission of poverty. Literature existed for three purposes: to teach what is useful, to honor what deserves honor, and to appreciate what is delightful. Authors were content to have their small role in the great pageant of history.[282]

"Few constructions of the imagination seem to me to have combined splendour, sobriety, and coherence in the same degree."[283] For Lewis, beyond anything, the model was imaginatively important. It influenced, as we have noted, his writing of the

279   Lewis, *The Discarded Image*, 203.
280   Lewis, *The Discarded Image*, 204–6.
281   Lewis, *The Discarded Image*, 204.
282   Lewis, *The Discarded Image*, 211.
283   Lewis, *The Discarded Image*, 216.

Ransom trilogy, *The Chronicles of Narnia*, and his poetry. If you read *The Discarded Image* and then the Narnia series, you will understand and see things in a way you couldn't before. Lewis loved this model so much that he imported many of its characteristics and ideas into this series. Once you gain knowledge of these things, it makes for an extremely rich reading experience.

In addition to the important impact on the arts of its time and its importance to Lewis, we can draw out of the medieval model three further influences that have profound implications for our own faith journeys. These include a vital understanding of the purpose of models, a proper humility, and a re-enchantment of our world.

Now, as Lewis notes, the medieval model was not ultimately true. In 1572, in the constellation of Cassiopeia, a supernova occurred which irrevocably altered the conception of the heavens. Prior to this, everything in the heavenly regions had been thought immutable, and observation had confirmed this. But this event proved that the heavens were *not* immutable, that change occurred in these regions just as it did on earth. It was this event and its ramifications that proved to be the parting valediction of the old model and the watershed moment for the birth of the modern sciences.

Thus, Lewis reminds us, all models must be provisional. They must also be metaphorical. It is all fine and well to say this model is not "true," he writes, but we have to be careful when we talk about the "truth" of models. In the nineteenth century, it was still believed that we could know ultimate physical reality by inferences from our sense experience: the truth of any given thing would be a mental replica of the thing itself. Today, on the other hand, the sciences and mathematics are seen to be the closest we can get to reality. But mathematics is not imaginable. Even the scientists must use models, must illustrate aspects of a truth by analogy.[284]

Lewis provides an example. Modern scientists talk about the "curvature of space." This is comparable to the medieval conception

284   Lewis, *The Discarded Image*, 216–18.

of God's immanence as "a circle whose centre is everywhere and whose circumference is nowhere," writes Lewis.[285] Both suggest things to our minds, but they are nonsense on the level of ordinary thinking. By accepting the modern understanding, or, really, metaphor, we aren't knowing or enjoying truth in the way it was once thought possible. What we know now, Lewis writes, is that we can't know, in the old sense, what the universe is really like. Thus, we suffer an imaginative loss. He suggests in his essay "Is Theology Poetry?" that all language is metaphorical:

> We can, if you like, say "God entered history" instead of saying "God came down to earth." But, of course, "entered" is just as metaphorical as "came down." You have only substituted horizontal or undefined movement for vertical movement. We can make our language duller; we cannot make it less metaphorical. We can make the pictures more prosaic; we cannot be less pictorial.[286]

So it is important to understand that regardless of the model, we are simply substituting one metaphor for another, and in the case of the change in metaphors from medieval to modern, there was a significant imaginative loss. The universe became less imaginable, more abstract, and more terrifying.

Lewis concludes by noting that we cannot dismiss the change in models as simply progress from error to truth. No model can ultimately explain reality, yet no model is a fantasy. All models seek to save the appearances given all the phenomena available at the time.[287] Each age must attempt to account for the facts, yet Lewis warns us that we must not idolize any given model, that at some point it will be superseded by new knowledge and will itself become a discarded image.

285   Lewis, *The Discarded Image*, 218.
286   Lewis, *The Weight of Glory*, "Is Theology Poetry?" (New York: Simon & Schuster, 1996), 102.
287   Lewis, *The Discarded Image*, 222.

Yet an imaginable universe was key to one's faith. Medievals packed their universe full of imaginative significance because they understood that the imagination is the primary way we can conceive of God. God is infinite. We can't define him with logic or reason. The word *definition* means "of the finite." We use words and language to help us understand reality. Therefore, God transcends the category of definition. We can't access an understanding of him through reason in the same way we can through imagination. That's why Jesus told parables using simile and metaphor. The kingdom of heaven is *like* a man who sowed good seed in his field. The kingdom of heaven is *like* treasure hidden in a field. The kingdom of heaven is *like* a man traveling to a far country. And so on. God is, in a sense, like mathematics. We need metaphors or models to understand his nature, to bring him down to the level of definition, in the finite world where we live. It brings a vast abstraction to the level of a concrete instance that, while not the thing itself, helps us grasp it, to get a clearer bearing on the "bright blur" as Lewis often referred to God. And the richer the metaphor, the richer our understanding.

A paucity of metaphors is characteristic of our modern age with its ambiguous and abstract metaphors that don't reach our imaginations. Perhaps we should do as Lewis suggests on a number of occasions and go for a walk on a dark, starlit night, resolutely assuming that pre-Copernican astronomy is, in fact, true. Lewis predicts that the true significance of the medieval universe will then begin to dawn on us. It will reawaken a sense of our place in the universe as well as re-enchant our imagination.

Medieval scholars and artists could teach us a humility that we don't often possess, if we would be open to it. Recall that the medieval author was content to reiterate, to tell again and again the story of the universe and the glory of God, to participate in a very small way in passing on its knowledge to others, to be satisfied with the tiny part he or she played. In an age of increasing self-aggrandizement and self-obsession where the idea of a historical continuum has been seriously eroded or possibly even expunged, we need that humility more than ever. Stories are not seen to be worthy of being reiterated without significant amendments, often by importing current divisive cultural issues and making them fit into narratives where they have no place. The world has contracted to the small sphere of the self and its constant promotion. We need the humility of the medieval imagination to keep us from thinking that this world, that *we*, are all that exists. It is only by ceding our power that we can allow God to be all-powerful and thus take our proper place in the scheme of things. And we desperately need a sense of perspective, of our small place in the long sweep of history.

Unfortunately, as it relates to history, we have held the view that every other age was less advanced than our own. Lewis calls this "chronological snobbery" and notes that it is:

> . . . the uncritical acceptance of the intellectual climate common to our own age and the assumption that whatever has gone out of date is on that account discredited. You must find why it went out of date. Was it ever refuted (and if so by whom, where, and how conclusively) or did it merely die away as fashions do? If the latter, this tells us nothing about its truth or falsehood. From seeing this, one passes to the realization that our own age is also "a period," and certainly has, like all periods, its own characteristic illusions. They are likeliest to lurk in those widespread assumptions which are so ingrained in the age that no one dares to attack or feels it necessary to defend them.[288]

It is plausible that Lewis may have written *The Discarded Image* for just this reason. To teach us the proper use of models, yes, but also to help us see what is important and beneficial in all models, and why a flat rejection of older models is a form of blindness that we carry into our current age where we are unable to accurately see

288   Lewis, *Surprised by Joy* (New York: Harcourt Brace & World, 1955), 207–8.

and judge current cultural and faith issues. Developing a critical skepticism to our own intellectual climate might be the antidote to this way of thinking, as this mindset takes the past into account. And to properly understand this past, we can utilize what Lewis called the historical imagination,[289] which helps reconstruct from available data what the conditions might have been like during some past period of time. This enables us to place ourselves into a historical period and better understand its literature and art.

G. K. Chesterton wrote that man must be an "heir of all the ages" in order to experience reality fully. He notes:

> Nevertheless, there are some of us who do hold that the metaphor of inheritance from human history is a true metaphor, and that any man who is cut off from the past, and content with the future, is a man most unjustly disinherited; and all the more unjustly if he is happy in his lot, and is not permitted even to know what he has lost. And I, for one, believe that the mind of man is at its largest, and especially at its broadest, when it feels the brotherhood of humanity linking it up with remote and primitive and even barbaric things. . . . Man should be a prince looking from the pinnacle of a tower built by his fathers, and not a contemptuous cad, perpetually kicking down the ladders by which he climbed.[290]

Even Isaac Newton famously said, "If I have seen further, it is by standing on the shoulders of giants." History gives us a kind of wise prescience, at least as it relates to trends and patterns. But Lewis warns us to be careful of sinking into what he calls *historicism*, the belief that by studying the past we can learn historical and transcendental truth. Lewis disagreed and believed this interfered with a true understanding of history.[291] One does, though, require

---

289   Lewis, *The Allegory of Love* (New York: Oxford University Press, 1953), 1.
290   G.K. Chesterton, *Avowals and Denials* (London: Methuen & Co., 1934), 74–78.
291   Lewis, *The Discarded Image*, 174.

the past to accurately understand and interpret the present. You can't divorce the one from the other without severe implications. However, a statement like this is heresy in our current cultural climate where the only thing that signifies is the ever-present, the immediate *now*. That's why *The Discarded Image* is so important. It gives us a window into the past, a way to inform and enrich our present. And once we have internalized the medieval worldview, it might give us new eyes and help re-enchant our own world.

Thus, the third influence that has important ramifications for our faith is the idea of re-enchantment. The old bromide that familiarity breeds contempt is entirely true. Not only do we not "see" the world around us because we encounter it constantly, our own age encourages us toward ideologies and habits of mind that darken our vision rather than bring clarity. The near total proliferation of screens and information is a major cause of our turning inward to such an extent that we are now constantly attentive to our devices, as if they needed to be looked after like a small child. Our ability to see the natural world and even people accurately has been seriously attenuated. How often do you see someone simply sitting and observing their world without the scrim of some device obscuring their vision of the wider world? The move to automate every aspect of life and the all-consuming drive for efficiency has led to an extreme reductionism that doesn't account for complexity, what Lewis called the roughness and density of life.

To counter this insidious cultural shift, we need to develop what Lewis terms the satisfied imagination.[292] This type of imagination delights in the familiar, simple, mundane, and repetitive in order to bring our minds back to the eternal source of order and repetition. This was the medieval mindset. It re-enchants the familiar by enabling us to see beyond the familiarity that breeds contempt to fresh perspectives and insight. It re-complexifies the world so that

292   Lewis, *The Discarded Image*, 203.

it becomes mysterious and unknowable, fresh and invigorating. Every branch, every tree, every passing cloud can, if we will let it, turn our minds back to the source of all creation: the Creator. We can find delight in the world by simply being glad that things are, rather than by diminishing their significance by reducing them to their constituent parts. We can embrace the medieval idea of plenitude and recapture a sense that the universe is crowded with God. Gerard Manley Hopkins embodies this superbly in his poem "God's Grandeur":

> The world is charged with the grandeur of God.
>> It will flame out, like shining from shook foil;
>> It gathers to a greatness, like the ooze of oil
> Crushed. Why do men then now not reck his rod?
> Generations have trod, have trod, have trod;
>> And all is seared with trade; bleared, smeared with toil;
>> And wears man's smudge and shares man's smell: the soil
> Is bare now, nor can foot feel, being shod.
>
> And for all this, nature is never spent;
>> There lives the dearest freshness deep down things;
> And though the last lights off the black West went
>> Oh, morning, at the brown brink eastward, springs—
> Because the Holy Ghost over the bent
>> World broods with warm breast and with ah! bright wings.[293]

---

293   Robert Bridges, ed., *Poems of Gerard Manley Hopkins* (New York: Oxford University Press, 1959), 70.

Chapter 8

A Defense of Old Ideas

Selected Literary Essays

Selected Literary Essays shows the breadth of Lewis's literary interests beyond medieval and Renaissance literature. Published in 1969, the book contains essays that were previously published elsewhere and brought together into one collection by editor Walter Hooper. In this volume are twenty-two essays on such topics as Shakespeare, Jane Austen, Sir Walter Scott, William Morris, and others. Additionally, there are several essays on literary critical method.

It is in this work that we most clearly see Lewis's efforts at *rehabilitation*. We mentioned in the introduction that Lewis was interested in defending and/or reconceptualizing certain periods, genres, and authors for which appreciation or critical understanding had been lacking. For example, in writing about Sir Walter Scott, he is mounting a defense of old ideas for an author who even in Lewis's time had been sadly neglected. And he found the criticism of Scott, in the main, to be misguided. So he chose, usually from love of a particular author or genre, to defend what he believed to be true about that literature. Often, he was working against evaluative criticism—the dominant criticism of his day—which pushed its judgments of literature on others. However, he advocated for a criticism that simply described a work as it was and left the judgments up to the readers.[294]

Because the nature of this work is so varied, this chapter will focus on two essays in this work that deal specifically with methodology. They are representative of Lewis's critical thought; the ideas they embody appear in some of Lewis's other work and are particularly meaningful to our own time and culture.

"De Descriptione Temporum"

This essay, the title of which translates to "a description of the times," was Lewis's inaugural lecture at Cambridge University as Professor of Medieval and Renaissance English Literature. Lewis was interested in explaining to his students the way in which he worked so they knew what to expect from him as a professor. He takes as his subject the ways in which the past has traditionally been divided into periods, particularly the idea that there was a great division that marked radical change from one era to another, a popular idea of his time. He calls this idea the Great Divide.

Lewis advocates the need for an increased flexibility in how one conceives of history. He notes that there are problems with the ways in which the past is divided. And for his own area of expertise, he suggests that the barrier between medieval and Renaissance literature has been exaggerated. He then avers that all

---

294   Lewis, *An Experiment in Criticism* (New York: Cambridge University Press, 2008), 120.

lines of demarcation between historical periods should be subject to constant revision. He is interested in understanding the best way to divide these periods that will falsify them the least. Historical periods are not facts and if we treat them as such, they will often lead us astray. He notes that the experience of the actual temporal process—the living of our own lives, and the only historical process we can experience—is not divided into periods.[295]

So Lewis, despite the fact that he didn't hold with the idea that there was some great division that marked radical change from one period to another in the past, still believed the question was worth asking because it would help his students understand his approach. Given that the real past is almost entirely inaccessible to us, Lewis nonetheless recognized the need for organizing those facts about history that we do possess.

He places the first major division of the past between antiquity and the Dark Ages. This period saw massive changes: the fall of the Roman Empire, barbarian invasions, and what he calls "the christening of Europe," that is, its conversion to Christianity. But then he notes that three things have happened since the mid-eighteenth century that make these changes seem less catastrophic. First, the partial loss of ancient learning and its recovery in the Renaissance were unique; this sort of thing had never happened before. But, Lewis notes, we have lived to see the second death of learning in our age. "In our time, something which was once the possession of all educated men has shrunk to being the technical accomplishment of a few specialists."[296]

Second, the perceived novelty of changes in literary taste during the division between antiquity and the Dark Ages seemed to be a big deal to historians, but Lewis suggests that modern writing offers the true novelty, that the differences in literature of the past

295 Lewis, *Selected Literary Essays*, "De Descriptione Temporum" (New York: Cambridge University Press, 1969), 2–3.
296 Lewis, *Selected Literary Essays*, 4.

offer no comparison to the novelty brought about by, say, T. S. Eliot's *The Waste Land*. It is a serious break from the continuity of literature in the past. Third, the christening of Europe was a unique event in history. But, Lewis suggests, we are witnessing the un-christening of Europe.

Our ancestors divided history into pre-Christian and Christian. Now, we must add a third category: post-Christian. The first two periods had something in common. In fact, Lewis notes that Christians and pagans had far more in common than is generally believed and certainly far more in common than either had with a post-Christian. He writes, "If I have ventured, a little, to modify our view of the transition from 'the Antique' to 'the Dark,' it is only because I believe we have since witnessed a change even more profound."[297]

Lewis's second major division of the past is placed between the Dark and Middle Ages, somewhere in the early twelfth century. During this time there was widespread improvement, including the recovery of Aristotle, architectural advances, and new literary forms. Yet again, Lewis writes, these changes pale in comparison with the novelty of poetry in the twentieth century.[298]

The third major division is drawn toward the end of the seventeenth century, around the time of Jane Austen and Sir Walter Scott. Here we see the advance of the sciences that was the beginning of all the vast changes to come. Lewis calls this the greatest of all the divisions in the history of the West.[299] This then is where he marks the Great Divide referred to earlier. He then presents a number of reasons for this conclusion. One reflects the change in political order between Scott's age and ours. It was the aim of rulers of the past, Lewis writes, to keep the people quiet and peaceful. But the aim of modern government is mass excitement.

297 Lewis, *Selected Literary Essays*, 4–5.
298 Lewis, *Selected Literary Essays*, 6.
299 Lewis, *Selected Literary Essays*, 7.

And there has been a significant change in language: from rulers to leaders. Lewis suggests that what one wants in a ruler is justice, incorruption, diligence, and so forth. But a leader is required to have dash, initiative, and charisma. This simple change in language illustrates a profound movement in thought. Another reason suggests there have been major changes in the arts. Lewis writes, "I do not think that any previous age produced work which was, in its own time, as shatteringly and bewilderingly new as that of the Cubists, the Dadaists, the Surrealists, and Picasso has been in ours."[300] For example, in ages past, most everyone agreed on what poetry meant; they all agreed on the answers to the puzzles that poetry presented. But now, assemble a number of adults in a room to talk about a T. S. Eliot poem and not one of them will agree on what it means. Again, Lewis suggests that "In the whole history of the West, from Homer—I might almost say, from the *Epic of Gilgamesh*—there has been no bend or break in the development of poetry comparable to this."[301]

Yet another reason is the religious changes that have taken place. He mentioned earlier the un-christening of Europe or the loss of Christianity. In the past some kind of faith or religious practice was the norm, even among pagans. Now it is the exception. As Lewis noted, we live in a post-Christian world.

Finally, Lewis unveils the greatest reason for his demarcation of the Great Divide: the birth of the machines. This change, he writes, is greater than any of the others. It is a change that alters man's place in nature. As a professor of literature, Lewis was concerned with the psychological effect of this change, seen most clearly in the ways language had altered. Words like *stagnation* or *primitive* that are used to disavow the past once had more positive meanings. Or how the word *latest* has come to mean *best*. Of this change in language through technical advances and their connection with

---

300 Lewis, *Selected Literary Essays*, 8.
301 Lewis, *Selected Literary Essays*, 9.

progress and betterment, Lewis says, "Assuredly that approach to life which has left these footprints on our language is the thing that separates us most sharply from our ancestors and whose absence would strike us as most alien if we could return to their world."[302] Note also Lewis's treatment of language change and its ramifications in the previous chapter on *Studies in Words*.

Let us recall that this essay was his inaugural lecture delivered at Cambridge University. After stating his reasons for marking the Great Divide in the modern era, Lewis then positions himself in relation to his students as a translator of Old Western Culture. This means that despite the fact that he taught medieval and Renaissance English literature, he would still need to bring in a lot of material regarding the times before and after his stated subject area, material that would help his students understand what it was like to live in that world.

But he hastens to reassure his students. He writes that the study of any historical period doesn't need to be seen as nostalgia or an enslavement to the past. Besides, it is not the remembered, but the forgotten past that enslaves us. He notes, "To study the past does indeed liberate us from the present, from the idols of our own market-place. But I think it liberates us from the past too."[303] He then informs his audience that he reads as a native, texts that they must read as foreigners. Thus, in order to read literature of the period he calls Old Western, they will have to suspend the responses and habits they have learned in reading modern literature.

Importance of this Essay

This essay reminds us of the fact that we're living through the biggest historical changes of the West, and Lewis wants us to know that the writers and thinkers of these periods of the past are vital to informing our present, to liberating us from the idols of our own

302   Lewis, *Selected Literary Essays*, 11.
303   Lewis, *Selected Literary Essays*, 12.

time. It gives us a sense of our current relation to history and the ways we are cut off from the past. It is, perhaps, not impossible, but it would take a herculean dissociation from our current mindsets to engage with history in the way Lewis asks of us. Yet, we must make the effort.

Perhaps a further explanation is needed. We have mentioned before the need for the historical imagination to be able to see the world through the eyes of other ages, so that we might see our present more clearly. This becomes increasingly difficult in an age of rapid change. In Lewis's day, there were significant technological changes, but they were nothing compared to the exponential escalation of today's technologies and the wholesale acceptance of them that have changed the way we experience the world and the way we think. Its values are anti-historical, as opposed to the experiment that Lewis is suggesting students could still make in 1960, but even then, only by a sharp dissociation. We have gone much further down the rabbit hole.

If we were able, through an inexplicable episode of time travel, to return to Lewis's Oxford of the 1940s and 1950s, we would enter a world at once slow and grainy and almost incomprehensible to our current mindsets and habits. Change comes upon us thick and fast. Constant change is the new constant. In our culture, if it doesn't change, it dies. Digital technologies run our lives to a large extent and this acquiescence or capitulation to our devices has, over time, changed the way we think. It has changed our relationship to time and space, and therefore to our understanding of history. This sort of rapid-fire technological advance makes it difficult to remember a past. Compared to the current change rate, even the recent past looks stodgy. The sort of literary study that was once possible (though well into decline even in Lewis's time) is no longer possible. To be clear, we can certainly still study the past and be enriched by it, but we can no longer dissociate our world from it. We can no longer suspend our responses and habits.

Cultural critic Sven Birkerts notes that "Media restructures our perceptions—we may produce people who know facts about the past, but have no purchase on 'pastness' itself."[304] Though he was writing in the 1990s on the cusp of the huge digital shift, his observations are still incisive and relevant: "For once the world goes fully on-line, there will be no more history of the old kind. History as we all studied it in school depended not just on the idea of chronological sequence, but also on fixed coordinates of space and time."[305] This is what makes an effort to use the historical imagination so difficult for us now.

For nearly two thousand years, change was of degree. It was slow in arriving. People could easily adapt to it. In less than thirty years we have turned that entire formula on its head. What we are living through now is a change of kind that not even Lewis, perhaps, could have anticipated. The rate of change is so intense that without conscious effort, we can no longer accommodate or keep up with it.

This is what we are up against as we think about the past. To examine these ideas further is beyond the scope of this book, but it needs to be mentioned since it is the reality in which we live, and we want to be careful to approach these things with our eyes open. In order to begin to understand what has been lost and forgotten, we first need to regain a sense of perspective. There is a tremendously rich and varied past that is vital for us to know. Again, Lewis would have us beware of chronological snobbery, of thinking that our own age is somehow better than others. This is our starting point.

Additionally, we somehow need to be able to step away from our habits of mind in order to access the past more fully. And we will be up against it in the effort. Deep habits of the contemporary mind include, among others, constant distraction, the inability to

304 Sven Birkerts, *The Gutenberg Elegies* (New York: Ballantine Books, 1994), 137.
305 Birkerts, *The Gutenberg Elegies*, 214.

focus or be quiet, the loss of the historical continuum, and constant stimulation. Most people will not see the need and even if they do, won't do anything about it. Unfortunately, it will only be for the few who are willing to undergo its rigors. And those rigors will not be inconsequential.

Finally, we should see the past as an interpreter of the present. In whatever way we can and to whatever degree, we need to study the past. Lewis himself provides the maps to some of these areas of Old Western culture. He has left behind books in which his thought on these subjects is distilled. He acts as a translator for us as well, so we may enter in. And as Lewis has noted before, it is old books that give us a standard by which to judge more modern works. They help correct the characteristic mistakes and blindness of our own period.

"Bluspels and Flalansferes: A Semantic Nightmare"

This essay was originally a lecture delivered at Manchester University and later published in Lewis's book *Rehabilitations*. His purpose was to understand the nature of what he called "dead metaphors" and how our thinking may be limited by them. Ultimately, he desired to understand how we can think more accurately.

To begin, he notes that there are two ways a metaphor can come into existence. First, in beginning with a concept that we don't understand, we may invent or find a new metaphor by luck or inspiration. Or someone else may enable us to understand through their metaphor. When this occurs, our new understanding is tied to the metaphor. It is a metaphor by which we are taught. Lewis calls this the Pupil's metaphor.

Second, to reverse the process, we may be attempting to explain a concept to someone who doesn't understand, and so be the one to create a metaphor. We use this metaphor as a temporary tool because we already possess a prior understanding of the concept.

We are able to use it and keep our thinking clear of it. It doesn't dominate us. We use it to teach. Lewis calls this the Master's metaphor.[306]

To attain some measure of truth from a Pupil's metaphor requires three things on the part of the teacher. First, that the metaphor should be well-chosen; if we don't see what we are meant to see accurately, we end by thinking nonsense. Second, that we get the exact imagery—that we understand it—and third that we realize the metaphor is a metaphor and not the thing it represents.[307]

Now that we understand how metaphors may come into being, Lewis returns to his original question of how these two relations (the effect on our thought of a Master's or Pupil's metaphor) change as metaphors age and die. Recall that what Lewis is attempting to understand is how we can think more clearly.

We'll begin with the Master's metaphor. To explain the philosophy of Kant to a hypothetical pupil, Lewis uses the following metaphor: "Kant answered the question 'How do I know that whatever comes around the corner will be blue?' by the supposition 'I am wearing blue spectacles.'"[308] This metaphor may continue to be used long after the master forgets its origins. The word may even change in his mind to *bluspels*. In this case, the forgetting will not affect the master's thinking about Kant because it was already in place prior to creating the metaphor for the pupil.[309]

To understand what occurs with the aging of a Pupil's metaphor, Lewis imagines a situation in which he, ignorant of mathematics, is instructed by a hypothetical master with a metaphor to help him understand the theory that space is finite. We live in three dimensions, so we cannot understand how space could be limited, but the metaphor will show us how it could be limited to someone

---

306 Lewis, *Selected Literary Essays*, "Bluspels and Flalansferes: A Semantic Nightmare," 252–55.
307 Lewis, *Selected Literary Essays*, 254.
308 Lewis, *Selected Literary Essays*, 255–56.
309 Lewis, *Selected Literary Essays*, 256.

who perceived reality in four dimensions. To this end, Lewis describes a race of Flatlanders who only know two dimensions and who live on a globe. He calls this the "flatlander's sphere."[310] He continues with the metaphor:

> And suppose they were living on a globe. They would have no conception, of course, that the globe was curved—for it is curved round in that third dimension of which they have no inkling. They will therefore imagine that they are living on a plane; but they will soon find out that it is a plane which nowhere comes to an end; there are no edges to it. Nor would they be able even to imagine an edge. For an edge would mean that, after a certain point, there would be nothing to walk on; nothing below their feet. But that below and above dimension is just what their minds have not got; they have only backwards and forwards, and left and right. They would thus be forced to assert that their globe, which they could not see as a globe, was infinite. You can see perfectly well that it is finite. And now, can you not conceive that as these Flatlanders are to you, so you might be to a creature that intuited four dimensions? Can you not conceive how that which seems necessarily infinite to your three-dimensional consciousness might none the less be really finite?[311]

The Pupil's metaphor can become fossilized in two ways. Recall that with this metaphor, thought is dominated by the metaphor. The pupil doesn't have a prior conception of the idea independent of the metaphor, unlike the Master's metaphor. Therefore, if I, as the pupil, become a mathematician, I can get beyond the metaphor. I no longer need it. This is the first way.

The second way this metaphor may age, Lewis writes, is if I remain ignorant of mathematics. Years later, the word Flatlanders

310   Lewis, *Selected Literary Essays*, 253–54.
311   Lewis, *Selected Literary Essays*, 254.

may have morphed into *flalansferes* and the imagery associated with it be forgotten. Unfortunately, the word was never known except through the imagery; I didn't get beyond it to the thing of which the imagery is only a copy. If I've lost the imagery, then, the word becomes meaningless. Lewis notes that we're not thinking when we use the word, but we don't know this. Thus the word can be used to fit various contexts. Meaning anything, it ultimately means nothing. Lewis sees this kind of fossilization of metaphors as the situation we are primarily in.[312]

He now throws a wrench into his inquiry. Even in using the Master's metaphor—which is the superior knowledge of a concept—we didn't pass from symbol to symbolized, but rather from one metaphor to another. For example, a mathematical equation is just as metaphorical as the "Flatlander's sphere." He has led us to believe that we had two methods of thought, the literal and the metaphorical. But now he writes that if you cast one metaphor aside, you must substitute it with another. This raises the question of whether or not we can truly know anything. Lewis notes that to have a choice of what metaphors we will use is to know more than we know when we are the slave to just one metaphor. All of our thought and our ability to describe or identify isn't as metaphorical as simply defining something. When we define, he writes, this only leads to a reshuffling of buried metaphors. So trying to think independently of a metaphor via a new apprehension just turns out to be metaphorical itself, or worse; it just becomes words enshrining ignored metaphors.[313]

For example, in medieval thought, gravity was conceived as "kindly enclyning." If you dropped a rock, it fell to the ground because it wanted to return to its natural environment, its home. Today we might say that gravity obeys certain laws. We have simply exchanged one metaphor for another. The things of which

312 Lewis, *Selected Literary Essays*, 257–58.
313 Lewis, *Selected Literary Essays*, 261–62.

we speak can never be apprehended literally. Lewis states that there are three possibilities here. We can have literalness, nonsense, or metaphor. Since we can't have the first and we don't want to talk without meaning, we must use the last.

In *Letters to Malcolm: Chiefly on Prayer*, Lewis avers that not even simple things like tables and chairs are explained by the words we use to describe them. They are simply metaphors we use to describe objects that are charged with appalling energies that we can't even begin to understand. Unless we could watch creation as it bursts directly from the hand of God, we can never go deep enough to apprehend the ultimate reality of anything. This doesn't mean that we cannot know anything; truth can always be more deeply understood. However, we cannot ever get to the bottom of it. And we can only speak through metaphor.[314] So we can use metaphors and think something, though less than we wish, or we can think nonsense by using unrecognized metaphors. For example, when we think of the Flatlanders and realize they are a metaphor for the conception that space is finite, we are in a superior position to someone who talks about *flalansferes* and thinks they are being literal and straightforward.[315]

Lewis is ultimately interested in understanding how we can increase meaning or decrease meaninglessness in our speech and writing. To do this, he avers, we must do two things: We must become conscious of the fossilized metaphors in words. This requires knowledge and leisure, things in short supply in our current culture. And second, we can freely use new metaphors that we ourselves create. This requires a certain imaginative ability. The second is more important than the first.

Lewis's argument leads him to conclude that we must be content with a modest quantity of thinking as the core of all our talking, and that we must use metaphor more cautiously. If we take

314 Lewis, *Letters to Malcolm*, 78–79.
315 Lewis, *Selected Literary Essays*, 263.

Lewis's essay to heart, we now have a new standard of criticism to apply to our own and others' thought. It may seem difficult to care about all this if what Lewis says is true, that meaninglessness is more prevalent than meaning. But he suggests that we should take courage now that we have the key to thinking about our metaphorical situation. We should also be prepared to act on this knowledge because it is so important.[316]

Also, real meaning may not always be found where we might expect. Lewis notes that meaninglessness is more prevalent in certain types of writing. We can see his humor showing itself here. He suggests that different disciplines have differing levels of meaning in their writing. He writes that one hundred percent of the syntax or verbiage of political, journalistic, psychological, and economics writing is masquerading as meaning. By contrast, only forty percent of the syntax of children's stories is masquerading as meaning. But, in his list of writers, it is the poets that take the highest place because it is among them that we find those who care more for old words and have the best instinct for new metaphors. Lewis wants to make clear, here, that he is not talking of truth, but meaning. Thus, he notes that he is not putting forth imagination as the organ of truth. For him, imagination is the organ of meaning. Reason is the organ of truth. Meaning is antecedent to truth—not its cause, but its condition. In order to have truth, we must have meaning, therefore we must have imagination. This is why the poets rank highest in Lewis's scale and this is why we must have metaphors. We cannot have truth without them.[317]

Toward Thinking Clearly

In reading through this essay, we might be surprised by Lewis's assertion that all language is metaphorical, that we can never be literal, that everything we think and say is simply provisional until

316 Lewis, *Selected Literary Essays*, 263–64.
317 Lewis, *Selected Literary Essays*, 265–65.

a better metaphor can explain it. In fact, we may be disheartened by this suggestion. Our first task, then, if we hold that what Lewis says is true, will be to adjust our understanding of language, and this requires a certain acceptance of our semantic situation. This kind of awareness is difficult at best, and many of us won't venture to go there. But if we will take the trouble to be aware, perhaps we will be more careful. At least, we will have a healthy doubt about things we say with assurance or conviction. If the awareness causes us to be more careful in how we think and speak, then it will have had a happy effect.

To this end, Lewis writes, we must first understand how to think clearly. To do this, he outlines some guiding principles. For example, he distinguishes between thinking and imagining. The things we think are usually different from how we imagine these things. Lewis notes that our thinking can be true even when the accompanying imaginative understanding is false. We usually are aware that the imaginings are false, if we think about it. Then he shows how our thinking can be true not only when it is associated with false images, but also when we mistakenly believe the false images to be true. And finally, when we talk about things that cannot be grasped with the five senses, we must talk metaphorically. That is, we must talk about things as if they could be grasped with the five senses.[318]

For people of faith, this has implications, especially as to how we symbolize it to ourselves. When we picture God, or heaven, or some other such idea that is outside our experience, Lewis notes, we come armed with all kinds of mental pictures, which themselves, though not perfectly accurate, don't impinge on our real understanding. And even if we choose to get rid of our current images, we can only ever substitute them for another metaphor or image, hopefully one that gives us a better understanding. Lewis writes, "If a man watches his own mind, I believe he will find that

318   Lewis, *Miracles* (New York: Macmillan, 1953), 86–89.

what profess to be specially advanced or philosophic conceptions of God are, in his thinking, always accompanied by vague images which, if inspected, would turn out to be even more absurd than the man-like images aroused by Christian theology."[319]

This enables us to see our faith as an imaginative exercise and understand that we apprehend God only through imaginative metaphors. God is infinite. We are finite. We cannot define God with words or with reason. The word "definition" means "of the finite." It enables us to describe things by their limitations. "They are so big, they weigh this much," etc. Thus, because God is infinite, he is outside the category of definition. We get at an understanding of God through metaphors. Recall that Jesus spoke in parables to describe the kingdom of heaven. These are simply metaphors or similes. The kingdom of heaven is like . . . a person who sowed good seed, treasure hidden in a field, a merchant seeking beautiful pearls, a man traveling to a far country, and so forth. They are simply things that suggest the idea of the kingdom of heaven. They are not the thing itself, but they are the only understanding we can get.

All of this suggests that one of the things we must do is to wake up and see our semantic situation more clearly. And this renewed vision is itself a spiritual exercise, because we will foster awareness of the metaphors that have perhaps been inhibiting us in some way from perceiving any given tract of spiritual reality.

As Lewis writes, new and better metaphors help us grasp a truth more effectively. This puts the onus not only on our imaginative ability, but also on our knowledge of what the imagination is. We must, therefore, have no part in an understanding of imagination as something simply "made-up." He says that imagining is something more than simply having mental images. When we imagine a particular thing, we have images in our mind that assist whatever the real imagining is. But we must take these images provisionally.

319 Lewis, *Miracles*, 90.

Once they have served their purpose, we drop them. For example, if I am imagining the city of Oxford, images of St. Mary's spire or the Radcliffe Camera might come into my mind. But these are not the only things that comprise the city of Oxford. They simply assist in my imagining of the city. If I focus too long on them or they become the only thing I can think of when I think of Oxford, then my imagination is impaired.[320]

Our imaginations give us bearings on reality in a way that reason cannot. Lewis makes it clear that when we think about reality outside of our five senses, then we must use metaphor. That is, we must use our imagination. For a word that has had many negative connotations associated with it, this will be difficult medicine for some to take. But we must make the effort. Our ability to think clearly depends on it.

---

320   Lewis, *Christian Reflections,* "The Language of Religion" (London: Geoffrey Bles, 1967), 138–39.

This iconic picture of Lewis captures him at the height of his career when his Narnian books were largely written and his work as a Christian apologist was well known.

Used by permission of the Marion E. Wade Center, Wheaton College, Wheaton, IL.

Bearings on the Bright Blur

Much of C. S. Lewis's best work, originating from the focus and precision of his academic life, is too often neglected today. That's why we wrote this book, and we assume that's why you have read this book.

Most people go to Lewis for his Narnian novels or his Christian apologetics. *The Lion, the Witch, and the Wardrobe* and *Mere Christianity* will continue to sell hundreds of thousands of copies every year all over the world for decades to come. May it be so. But few people turn to his literary work.

But in the works discussed in the preceding chapters, we hope it has become clear that readers can discover things in Lewis that were previously beyond their grasp. This does not mean these things must remain permanently beyond reach. Lewis opens more than wardrobe doors. These literary texts lead to the long-lost worlds of Spenser's *The Fairie Queene*, Milton's *Paradise Lost*, Mallory's Arthurian lore, Chaucer's *Troilus and Cressida*, and a treasure trove of other great works that are part of our literary past, and that are keys to better understanding much of Lewis's popular work.

Entering the literary world at Lewis's invitation may reveal some degree of awkwardness, but all growth is preceded by moments of disequilibrium. The five-year-old taking the training wheels off the two-wheeler falls down and scrapes his knee. Remember when you went from the experience of elementary school to the multi-subject, multifaceted, confusing life of middle school? You had five minutes for passage from classroom to classroom, attempting along the way to work a locker whose combination seemed constantly to stick. Eventually you were able to do it with ease. All new experience reveals a level of awkwardness. In fact, if you are not awkward someplace in your life you are simply not growing.

We will never actually have a wardrobe door open that allows us to enter the world of Narnia. But Lewis holds open the door to the best of the books that have captured his imagination, and the attention of generations of others before him. Imagine coming into a new world, as Dante entered the *Inferno* with Virgil for a guide. Or the *Paradiso*, guided by Beatrice. In the world Lewis offers to his readers in these neglected books, he volunteers to be their guide. It is like Mr. Tumnus or the Beavers escorting us through Narnia, or Ransom guiding us through the space novels. Lewis proves to be a good guide, capable of opening up worlds that will give you a lifetime of enjoyment.

When he writes of the complexities of God and his world, he notes that we should always be taking bearings on the Bright Blur, that it might become brighter and less blurry.[321] Lewis writes about a variety of things to avoid if one wants to break out of the dungeon of self to discover a wider world. These cautions are drawn primarily from the neglected books that are discussed in the chapters above.

321 Lewis, *Letters to Malcolm*, 119.

But allow us to quickly offer just a few more examples.

The Personal Heresy may be Lewis's earliest attempt to speak against subjectivism, or self-referentialism, in literary criticism. He points out that some miss the objective text altogether by projecting onto it a quest for the author as opposed to the study of the text itself. Lewis warned against such literary practices. While this warning against subjectivism begins in *The Personal Heresy*, he continues to warn against this tendency right up to the publication of *An Experiment in Criticism*, nearly his last literary critical work. His warnings, when properly attended to, not only strengthen the ability to connect with the real world, but also become a spiritual exercise enabling one to live in the truth.

An Experiment in Criticism is where Lewis warns against the practice of "reading between the lines." This occurs when the critic fails to deal with the actual lines of a literary text, choosing rather to project onto the text what is not there at all. In reading between the lines, we show that we cannot read what is actually in the lines themselves. We become nearsighted. Again, the critic's world does not widen; rather, it contracts.

In *A Preface to Paradise Lost*, Lewis warns against what he calls "The Doctrine of the Unchanging Human Heart." He believed that because we have a shared humanity with any author from any time, we are therefore always proximate to what the author intended. Prehistoric man left no written records, but he did paint pictures on the walls of caves. We do not know why. Were these caves places of primitive worship and the paintings a sort of iconography? Were the paintings decorations for the walls of a communal nursery where children were entertained by the pictures as the men and women engaged in hunting and gathering food? Were the pictures decorations for a cave that celebrated the heroics of past hunts as well as fortified the courage of those who were about to face dangers in the field? What purpose the paintings served remains a mystery. Nevertheless, the fact that the paintings exist reminds us

162 • *The Neglected C. S. Lewis*

that whatever the differences, prehistoric people were artists. And if that is so, then to some degree they were not much different from us. The assumption is then that we can come to any text with our present grasp of a thing believing that out of our shared humanity we know what the author was driving at. Lewis says that while the humanity is shared, the remarkable thing about us is not what we have in common but how different we can be from age to age. It is the elasticity of what it means to be human that must also be respected. If we simply project onto the text our present cultural understanding, we will miss the intent of the author. And once again we will be fenced in and prevented from discovery of a wider world. Books, properly read, allow us to see beyond our present grasp and breathe the ambient air of a wider world.

Lewis also warns in his neglected works against chronological snobbery. This grows out of the assumption that whatever is newest must, on that basis alone, be better than what preceded it. Isaac Newton observed that "If I have seen further than others it was while sitting on the shoulders of giants." In many quarters such humility is dying. Our age is nearly characterized by the sentiment "It is amazing how far we have seen given the pigmies that preceded us." Chronological snobbery looks at the past as less refined and primitive and therefore in need of being superseded. To be sure, history is a pruning process. Nevertheless, it is the dead wood that must be pruned. That which has borne the fruit of wisdom for generations must be preserved and embraced for all wanting to inherit the riches of the past. When we look down on authors who preceded us without consideration of the actual literary merit of these authors, we have committed chronological snobbery. These neglected works of Lewis provide an antidote to such arrogance.

Several other warnings against entering the dungeon of self-reference can be found in the neglected works. Some of the most noteworthy would include "Historicism," "Psycho-analysis and Literary Criticism," "The Anthropological Approach" to literary criticism, and that form of criticism Lewis warns is found "at the Fringe of Language." Historicism is that belief that people "can by means of their natural powers, discover an inner meaning in the historical process."[322] Lewis challenged such thinking by noting, "I have no notion what stage in the journey we have reached. Are we in Act I or Act V? Are our present diseases those of childhood or senility?"[323] Psychoanalysis and literary criticism occur when the critic turns attention away from the text *per se* and seeks to analyze the psychology of the author. The author is not available to sit on our couch, and in most cases we are not psychologists. Charges such as narcissist, racist, Marxist, and so forth become little more than projection and thereby avoid what is actual and objectively present in the text.[324] Another error Lewis warns against in these neglected works is "the Anthropological Approach." This occurs when the critic turns attention away from the text itself and instead enters into a discussion as to how he or she conceives the text came to be written. These anthropological reconstructions are often amiss, and they are certainly a distraction leading away from an analysis of the actual text. The critic's imagination is engaged, but the text is left untouched. Subjectivism prevails.[325] Finally, "At the Fringe of Language" is a designation Lewis gives to circumstances where the critic tells the reader nothing about the text but only about his likes and dislikes. He or she never sets forth whether or not such likes and dislikes are merited by the text itself. All attention is riveted on the critic, and the text fades into obscurity.[326]

In these books that make up *The Neglected C. S. Lewis* one encounters an open door into a body of literature that leads out of the self and into a wider world. Lewis's critical tradition is similar to that of Matthew Arnold, who embraced the idea that the role

322 Lewis, *Christian Reflections*, 100.
323 Lewis, *Christian Reflections*, 106.
324 Lewis, *Selected Literary Essays*, 286–300.
325 Lewis, *Selected Literary Essays*, 301–11.
326 Lewis, *Studies in Words*, 214–32.

of the critic is to get himself out of the way and let the audience decide. Lewis's method is to describe well the texts before him. He rivets his readers' attention on what is there. He gives them the material by which they may assess whether or not his judgment is sound because the texts affirm what he has said about them. This practice, to one degree or another, is modeled throughout Lewis's professional life as a literary critic.

Fellow Inkling and literary critic Charles Williams once wrote, "Not one mind in a thousand can be trusted to state accurately what its opponent says, much less what he thinks."[327] Furthermore, Oxford University philosopher and professor Basil Mitchell, quoting John Locke, observed, "Whatsoever credit or authority we give to any proposition more than it receives from the principles and proofs it supports itself on, is owing to our inclination that way."[328] It is this kind of objectivity one learns to practice while reading these neglected books by Lewis. This is of great importance. We who read Lewis become his students and he our tutor. He once said to his students who were reading classic texts that "We have fulfilled our whole duty to you if we help you see some given tract of reality."[329] Lewis's literary criticism rescues his readers from literary ventriloquism.

327 Charles Williams, *The Descent of the Dove*, 112.
328 Basil Mitchell quoting John Locke, "Newman as Philosopher" in *Newman after a Hundred Years*, Ian Ker and Alan Hill, eds. (Oxford: Clarendon Press, 1990), 223.
329 Lewis, *Rehabilitations*, "On the English Syllabus" (New York: Oxford University Press, 1939), 87.

Acknowledgments

Mark would like to thank his wife, Reba, for her love and patience during the writing of this book; Jerry is grateful to his wife, Claudia Root, who has endured discussions about C. S. Lewis as well as travels all over the world, hearing lectures on Lewis-related topics for 45 years; she has been a valuable source of insight in all of my writing endeavors.

This book grew out of a series of lectures that were delivered at the Marion E. Wade Center at Wheaton College. Therefore, it is fitting to express gratitude to those at the Wade who have served so many engaged in Lewis research: David and Crystal Downing, Marjorie Lamp Mead, Mary Lynn Uitermarkt, Laura Schmidt, Elaine Hooker, Aaron Hill, Shawn Mrakovich, and Hope Grant. The authors are also grateful to the Wade Center for permission to use the Lewis images in this book.

In many ways these lectures were conceived during late-night discussions around the fire at the Brotherhood of the Briar, so a word of thanks is necessary to that Thursday evening gathering of friends and contemplatives. The authors also thank the 1405's for supplying the philosophic wine.

No book can be properly written in isolation of critical response and reflection. Jerry's chapters were read and critiqued by the Mead Men: Lon Allison, Walter Hanson, David Henderson, and Rick Richardson. Jerry is deeply grateful to them for the hours of listening and commenting on this manuscript as it was being written. Jerry also benefitted from lengthy discussions with Dr. Olga Lukmanova of Nizhy Novgorod Linguistics University about C. S. Lewis and the influences on his life and writing. He is also grateful for critical insights that have come from other close friends: Dr. Tim Tremblay, Professors Robert Bishop, Jeff Davis, Mark Lewis, Peter Walters, and David Sveen. He also acknowledges students in his Wheaton College small groups with whom he discussed the contents in this book: Amy Ahrenholz, Belle Bryant, Nia Buker, Sarah Dammarful, Maddie English, Biiftuu Gobena, Ellie Laymon, Jack Stradinger, Sophie Stradinger, Abbey Ticknor, Maddie Vonk, Kodie Warnell, and Abby Yoh. Jerry also thanks the Hume Lake chapter of the Brotherhood of the Briar: Tim and Deena Hoelzel, and Emma and Sarah; Tommy and Cassia Ferrara; Randy and Nancy Gruendyke; Erik and Donna Thoennes. Jerry is always grateful to Tim and Amy LeFever for the use of "Bearings" at Bodega Bay, where his chapters were largely written, and to his sister Kathy Hamlin, who first told him about C. S. Lewis.

Mark thanks Matthew Farrelly for his friendship, insight, and shared interest in all things related to Lewis; David Haskins for productive brainstorming sessions; Justin Conrad for all the years of friendship and support; and Jerry Root for an excellent collaboration and a longstanding friendship.

And finally, the authors are grateful for the folks at Paraclete Press, particularly Jon Sweeney, who saw the potential of the book and brought it to fruition, our copyeditor Robert Edmonson for his careful attention to the manuscript and Rachel McKendree for all her work in promoting the book.

Appendix

Additional Neglected Works of C. S. Lewis

The student of Lewis who is interested in studying his literary critical output in more depth will find here brief outlines of additional works not covered in this book. We hope they lead you to an even deeper knowledge and appreciation of Lewis as well as the literature that he loved.

A Preface to Paradise Lost

Originally delivered as the Ballard Matthews lectures at University College of North Wales, Lewis wrote this work as an introduction to John Milton's epic poem *Paradise Lost*. In the conclusion he writes, "The purpose of these lectures has been mainly 'to hinder hindrances' to the appreciation of *Paradise Lost*. . . ."[330] In it, he outlines primary and secondary epic, gives a defense for this particular style, looks at common misconceptions about the poem, does an analysis of Augustine's influence on Milton, and looks at several theological concepts embedded in the poem. He concludes with an estimate of the poem's value.

Image and Imagination

This book collects all of Lewis's book reviews, forty-two in all, written over thirty-five years. It also includes four additional essays. Editor Walter Hooper has organized the book into six sections of broad themes, including general discussions of literature, reviews of the work of his fellow Inklings, aspects of Christianity, classical literature, medieval and Renaissance literature, and Milton and later English literature. Hooper notes that "This book will

330   Lewis, *A Preface to Paradise Lost*, 125.

appeal principally to anyone with general interests in literature and religion, as well as those who have a particular regard for the academic work of C. S. Lewis, or who simply like good English prose style."[331]

Of Other Worlds

This book of nine essays examines Lewis's love of story, especially fairy tales and science fiction. Any who would understand why Lewis regarded the use of story so highly must be familiar with this book. The work also includes three science fiction short stories, the only short stories by Lewis ever to be published, and five chapters of a novel he was working on when he passed away.

Rehabilitations

Published in 1939, this is Lewis's earliest collection of essays to come under common cover. The book is rare and often difficult to come by. Most of the essays have now been republished. Peculiar to this book are Lewis's lectures "The Idea of an English School" and "Our English Syllabus," both delivered to the English faculty at Oxford University at the beginning of his career as an Oxford don. While these lectures came early in Lewis's career, much of his mature thought in literary criticism can be seen in germ in this book.

Spenser's Images of Life

This book began as lectures delivered at Cambridge University. Lewis had intended to turn the lectures into a book but passed away before he was able to do so. Alastair Fowler, a former student of Lewis and a Spenser scholar and Fellow of Brasenose College, Oxford University, was asked to turn Lewis's lecture notes into a book. It examines the proper response to Spenser's poem *The Faerie Queene* so that we will not misunderstand what the author

---

331 Lewis, *Image and Imagination* (New York: Cambridge University Press, 2013), xii.

meant when we read it. Lewis shows that much of the work must be understood as pageant, or the iconographical conveyance of meaning.

Studies in Medieval and Renaissance Literature

Compiled of the unpublished essays on medieval and Renaissance literature that editor Walter Hooper was able to find after Lewis's death, this book examines a number of subjects including the imagination and thought of the Middle Ages, essays on Dante and Spenser, as well as an essay on variation in Shakespeare and Milton's *Comus*. Readers who have already delighted in *The Discarded Image* will find this book indispensable to further study of the medieval and Renaissance periods.

They Asked for a Paper

Published in 1962, a year before Lewis's death, this work is a collection of essays that he put together for this publication. It includes essays in literary criticism such as "De Descriptione Temporum," "Hamlet: The Prince or the Poem?," "Kipling's World," "The Literary Impact of the Authorized Version," and others. He also wrote essays on matters of faith and practice such as "On Obstinacy in Belief," "Is Theology Poetry?," "The Weight of Glory," and others. The common thread running through these various topics is the integration of faith and learning, or faith seeking understanding.

Bibliography

Athanasius, Saint. *St. Athanasius on the Incarnation: The Treatise De Incarnatione Verbi Dei.* London: A.R. Mowbray, 1963.

Birkerts, Sven. *Changing the Subject: Art and Attention in the Internet Age.* Minneapolis: Graywolf, 2015.

Birkerts, Sven. *The Gutenberg Elegies: The Fate of Reading in an Electronic Age.* Boston: Faber and Faber, 1994.

Cantor, Norman F. *Inventing the Middle Ages: The Lives, Works, and Ideas of the Great Medievalists of the Twentieth Century.* Cambridge, UK: The Lutterworth Press, 1991.

Chesterton, G. K. *Avowals and Denials: A Book of Essays.* London: Methuen & Co., Ltd., 1934.

Chesterton, G. K. *Collected Works.* Vol. 6. San Francisco: Ignatius Press, 1991.

Como, James. *C. S. Lewis at the Breakfast Table, and Other Reminiscences.* New York: Macmillan, 1979.

Dante Alighieri. *The De Monarchia of Dante Alighieri.* Boston and New York: Houghton, Mifflin and Company, The Riverside Press, 1904.

Drayton, Michael. *Poems of Michael Drayton.* London: George Newnes, 1905.

Edwards, Bruce L. *C. S. Lewis: Life, Works, and Legacy.* Westport, CT: Praeger, 2007.

Edwards, Bruce L. *The Taste of the Pineapple: Essays on C.S. Lewis as Reader, Critic, and Imaginative Writer.* Bowling Green, KY: Bowling Green State University Popular Press, 1988.

Hooper, Walter. *C. S. Lewis: A Companion & Guide.* London: HarperCollins, 1996.

Hopkins, Gerard Manley. *Poems of Gerard Manley Hopkins.* London: Oxford University Press, 1948.

Hutchins, Robert Maynard. *The Great Books of the Western World.* Vol. 21. Chicago: Encyclopedia Britannica, 1952.

Jacobs, Alan. *The Pleasures of Reading in an Age of Distraction.* New York: Oxford University Press, 2011.

Ker, I. T. *Newman after a Hundred Years.* Oxford: Clarendon Press, 1990.

Lewis, C. S. *A Grief Observed.* New York: Harper Collins, 1994.

Lewis, C. S. *An Experiment in Criticism.* Cambridge: Cambridge University Press, 2008.

Lewis, C. S. *A Preface to Paradise Lost: Being the Ballard Matthews Lectures: Delivered at Univ. College, North Wales, 1941.* London: Oxford University Press, 1954.

Lewis, C. S. *Arthurian Torso: Containing the Posthumous Fragment of The Figure of Arthur.* London: Oxford University Press, 1948.

Lewis, C. S. *Christian Reflections.* Walter Hooper, ed. London: Geoffrey Bles, 1967.

Lewis, C. S. *English Literature in the Sixteenth Century Excluding Drama: The Completion of the Clark Lectures, Trinity College, Cambridge, 1944.* Oxford: Clarendon Press, 1954.

Lewis, C.S., ed. *Essays Presented to Charles Williams.* Grand Rapids, MI: Eerdmans, 1966.

Lewis, C. S., ed. *George MacDonald: An Anthology.* New York: HarperCollins, 2001.

Lewis, C. S. *God in the Dock: Essays on Theology and Ethics.* Walter Hooper, ed. Grand Rapids, MI: Eerdmans, 1970.

Lewis, C. S. *Letters to Malcolm: Chiefly on Prayer.* New York: Harcourt, Brace & World, 1964.

Lewis, C. S. *Mere Christianity.* London: Geoffrey Bles, 1953.

Lewis, C. S. *Miracles: A Preliminary Study.* New York: Macmillan, 1953.

Lewis, C. S. *Of Other Worlds: Essays and Stories*. New York: Harcourt, Brace & World, 1966.

Lewis, C. S. *Rehabilitations and Other Essays*. New York: Oxford University Press, 1939.

Lewis, C. S. *Selected Literary Essays*. New York: Cambridge University Press, 1969.

Lewis, C. S. *Studies in Medieval and Renaissance Literature*. Walter Hooper, ed. New York: Cambridge University Press, 2007.

Lewis, C. S. *Studies in Words*. New York: Cambridge University Press, 1967.

Lewis, C. S. *Surprised by Joy: The Shape of My Early Life*. New York: Harcourt, Brace & World, 1955.

Lewis, C. S. *The Abolition of Man, or, Reflections on Education with Special Reference to the Teaching of English in the Upper Forms of Schools*. Las Vegas, NV: Lits, 2012.

Lewis, C. S. *The Allegory of Love: A Study of Medieval Tradition*. New York: Oxford University Press, 1953.

Lewis, C. S. *The Discarded Image; an Introduction to Medieval and Renaissance Literature*. New York: Cambridge University Press, 1964.

Lewis, C. S. *The Great Divorce: A Dream*. London: Geoffrey Bles, The Centenary Press, 1945.

Lewis, C. S. *The Horse and His Boy*. London: Geoffrey Bles, 1961.

Lewis, C. S. *The Personal Heresy, a Controversy*. New York: Oxford University Press, 1939.

Lewis, C. S. *The Problem of Pain*. New York: Macmillan, 1962.

Lewis, C. S. *The Weight of Glory and Other Addresses*. New York: Simon & Schuster, 1996.

Lewis, C. S. *Undeceptions: Essays on Theology and Ethics*. Walter Hooper, ed. London: Geoffrey Bles, 1971.

Milton, John. *The Complete Poetical Works of John Milton*. Boston: Houghton Mifflin Company, 1924.

Morozov, Evgeny. *To Save Everything, Click Here: The Folly of Technological Solutionism*. New York: PublicAffairs, 2013.

Pieper, Josef. *Abuse of Language, Abuse of Power*. San Francisco: Ignatius Press, 1992.

Smith, D. Nichol, ed. *Essays and Studies: By Members of the English Association*. Vol. XIX. Oxford: Clarendon Press, 1934.

Tillyard, E. M. W. *Studies in Milton*. London, Chatto & Windus, 1930.

van der Laan, J. M. "Plastic Words: Words Without Meaning," *Bulletin of Science, Technology & Society*, 21, no. 5, 2001.

Waldock, Arthur John Alfred. *Paradise Lost and Its Critics*. Gloucester, MA: Peter Smith, 1959.

Weaver, Richard M. *The Ethics of Rhetoric*. Chicago, H. Regnery Co., 1953.

Williams, Charles. *The Descent of the Dove: A Short History of the Holy Spirit in the Church*. Grand Rapids, MI: Eerdmans, 1974.

Index

Scripture References

About Paraclete Press

WHO WE ARE

As the publishing arm of the Community of Jesus, Paraclete Press presents a full expression of Christian belief and practice—from Catholic to Evangelical, from Protestant to Orthodox, reflecting the ecumenical charism of the Community and its dedication to sacred music, the fine arts, and the written word. We publish books, recordings, sheet music, and video/DVDs that nourish the vibrant life of the church and its people.

WHAT WE ARE DOING

BOOKS | PARACLETE PRESS BOOKS show the richness and depth of what it means to be Christian. While Benedictine spirituality is at the heart of who we are and all that we do, our books reflect the Christian experience across many cultures, time periods, and houses of worship.

We have many series, including *Paraclete Essentials*; *Paraclete Fiction*; *Paraclete Poetry*; *Paraclete Giants*; and for children and adults, *All God's Creatures*, books about animals and faith; and *San Damiano Books*, focusing on Franciscan spirituality. Others include *Voices from the Monastery* (men and women monastics writing about living a spiritual life today), *Active Prayer*, and new for young readers: *The Pope's Cat*. We also specialize in gift books for children on the occasions of Baptism and First Communion, as well as other important times in a child's life, and books that bring creativity and liveliness to any adult spiritual life.

The MOUNT TABOR BOOKS series focuses on the arts and literature as well as liturgical worship and spirituality; it was created in conjunction with the Mount Tabor Ecumenical Centre for Art and Spirituality in Barga, Italy.

MUSIC | The PARACLETE RECORDINGS label represents the internationally acclaimed choir *Gloriæ Dei Cantores*, the *Gloriæ Dei Cantores Schola*, and the other instrumental artists of the *Arts Empowering Life Foundation*.

Paraclete Press is the exclusive North American distributor for the Gregorian chant recordings from St. Peter's Abbey in Solesmes, France. Paraclete also carries all of the Solesmes chant publications for Mass and the Divine Office, as well as their academic research publications.

In addition, PARACLETE PRESS SHEET MUSIC publishes the work of today's finest composers of sacred choral music, annually reviewing over 1,000 works and releasing between 40 and 60 works for both choir and organ.

VIDEO | Our video/DVDs offer spiritual help, healing, and biblical guidance for a broad range of life issues including grief and loss, marriage, forgiveness, facing death, understanding suicide, bullying, addictions, Alzheimer's, and Christian formation.

Learn more about us at our website
www.paracletepress.com
or phone us toll-free at 1.800.451.5006

SCAN
TO
READ

You may also be interested in...

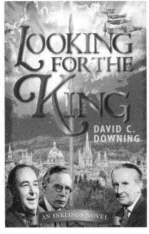

Looking for the King
An Inklings Novel
David C. Downing
ISBN 978-1-64060-349-3 | $17.99 | Trade paperback

"From the wild opening to the surprising ending, *Looking for the King* is the story of a fearless quest that crosses paths with our most beloved authors. Lewis and Tolkien both crackle to life with wit and intelligence. Dr. David Downing's prose delights and enchants as he asks and answers the important questions of our lives while also solving a great mystery. I felt as if I had walked into Oxford and then settled into the pub to spy on the Inklings in action—how grand! A novel you won't want to put down, and won't want to end."

—**Patti Callahan Henry**, *New York Times* best-selling author of *Becoming Mrs. Lewis*

A Well of Wonder
Essays on C. S. Lewis,
J. R. R. Tolkien, and The Inklings

Clyde S. Kilby
Edited by Loren Wilkinson and
Keith Call

ISBN 978-1-61261-862-3 | $28.99 | Hardcover

The Arts and the Christian Imagination
Essays on Art, Literature,
and Aesthetics

Clyde S. Kilby
Edited by William Dyrness and
Keith Call

ISBN 978-1-61261-861-6 | $28.99 | Hardcover